Lugano Holiday

Virginia C. Taylor

TRAFFORD

© Copyright 2003 Virginia C. Taylor. All rights reserved.

No part of this publication may be reproduced, stored in a retrieval system, or transmitted, in any form or by any means, electronic, mechanical, photocopying, recording, or otherwise, without the written prior permission of the author.

National Library of Canada Cataloguing in Publication Data

Taylor, Virginia C.
 Lugano holiday / Virginia C. Taylor.

ISBN 1-55395-825-X
 I. Title.
PS3620.A947L84 2003   813'.6   C2003-900962-9

TRAFFORD

This book was published *on-demand* in cooperation with Trafford Publishing.
On-demand publishing is a unique process and service of making a book available for retail sale to the public taking advantage of on-demand manufacturing and Internet marketing.
On-demand publishing includes promotions, retail sales, manufacturing, order fulfilment, accounting and collecting royalties on behalf of the author.

Suite 6E, 2333 Government St., Victoria, B.C. V8T 4P4, CANADA
 Phone   250-383-6864   Toll-free   1-888-232-4444 (Canada & US)
 Fax   250-383-6804   E-mail   sales@trafford.com
 Web site www.trafford.com   TRAFFORD PUBLISHING IS A DIVISION OF TRAFFORD HOLDINGS LTD.
 Trafford Catalogue #03-0188   www.trafford.com/robots/03-0188.html

10   9   8   7   6   5   4

Dedication

I dedicate this book to the memory of my grandmother
Anna Albertina Vonwiller

who was born on February 6, 1856 in St. Gallen, Switzerland.

To acknowledge all of the Swiss friends
who have helped to acquaint me with the country of my
grandmother's origin
are too numerous to mention.

Preface

In the southern-most part of Switzerland, lain like a jewel on blue-green velvet, lies the region of Lugano. Italian in flavor, yet decidedly Swiss, the charming town and distinctive hills surrounding the lake, have—for centuries—been a mecca for "... Going on Holiday."

My first visit to Switzerland occurred in 1951, when this country of my paternal ancestors celebrated its six-hundredth anniversary. Then, my "Lugano Holiday" lasted three days. Once—while strolling along the quay—I overheard conversation between two men seated on a bench. One was perhaps eighty; the other thirty years of age.

"Great spot for a honeymoon," said the young man wistfully.

"Humph," scoffed the elder, sweeping wide his arm. "Should never waste this on a honeymoon. Here... one should fall in love!

Because I had fallen in love with Lugano itself, I returned more recently; for a longer stay.

One evening as I stood on the balcony outside my room, I watched two lovers seated on, perchance, the same bench—now painted bright red. In the twilight, their silhouette appeared as one image, for her head nestled against his shoulder in the protection of his arm.

In the days to follow I learned that the man had come from Gloucester, in Massachusetts and the girl from the old city of Zürich. Her room was down the hall from mine, and we often spoke to each other. She was a warm, open person whose likeness could have graced a travel poster. It was most delightful to be drawn into the magic of her friendliness.

One rainy morning she entered the dining room alone and I asked her to join me at breakfast. She told me that, although she was hopelessly in love with the tall American, at weeks-end they would part. "My father," she added sadly, "would never allow us to marry."

"A flimsy excuse," I retorted impatiently. "No one could keep you apart, if <u>you</u> were truly in love."

"Oh, but I am!" she cried, her voice rising in rebellious anger.

Yet, it was not defiance which flared in her dark blue eyes. Their fiery depths were spread fiercely wide, like those of an animal caught in a trap. She had continued then with a strange story, which I found difficult to believe.

Several days later, on the afternoon of her departure, an odd thing happened. I answered a knock at my door, and for the moment saw only a large white vase filled with blood-red roses. Before I could respond, the vase was thrust into my hands. I caught only a glimpse of thick brown hair as the donor turned and hurried away.

Although her name was quite different, it seems fitting that I should call her… Rosina.

Chapter 1

Rosina Wyler, assistant secretary in Foreign Correspondence at Siegwart Freres, Zurich, stood at the office window staring absently across the courtyard, three stories below. In the circle of her left arm. she cradled a heavy notebook, supporting it loosely with her right hand, where, from between tense fingers, protruded a red pencil. The pencil matched the color of her short skirt. And the blouse above it, demurely white, set off the luxurious softness of dark brown, gently waving hair. She watched beneath her as figures moved across the pavement; two engaged in animated conversation; others going singly from one building to another. Her attention was drawn to a flag being hoisted up beside the familiar white cross on a crimson ground—proud symbol of her native Switzerland. This one—red and white striped with a blue field of stars—instilled in her the knowledge that the Company had visitors from the United States. Yesterday, Australia's fluttered there; last week, Costa Rica's and Brazil's. All visitors to Siegwart Freres, the company of Rosina's employment.

With wistful longing, Rosina visioned these exciting, romantic places which she had never seen. Tangible contact with them came only through the multilingual letters she translated and the ever-changing flags whipping against the pole.

In her student years she had studied languages avidly, day-dreaming imaginative visits to distant lands. Now, years later, the day-dreams had become as nebulous as drifting clouds which dispersed forever with each day's setting sun. Her talent had proved to be a vital asset within the vast combine of Siegwart Freres—a leading manufacturer of heavy power equipment—whose markets reached the far-flung corners of the earth.

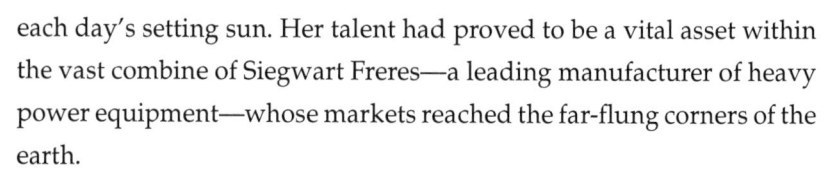

Behind her, typewriters clacked in unmelodious rhythm, while from outlying buildings, muffled sounds of humming motors, whirring lathes, the whish of hydraulic lifts, and the clang of cranes, merged consistently into never-ending sonorescence. Within the droning repetition she seemed to hear—over and over and over—the catechism of her life. Her father's oft-spoken command, "Do as you are told." "Why, Vati?" "Because I say so!" Echoed by the mother's docile, "Do as Vati tells you." "Why, Mutti?" "Simply because he is your father."

At times she became so disembodied, invisible cords seemed to bind her arms, leaden weights appeared to replace her shoes, and a deathly chill, like icy water coursed rampant through her veins. Dissent caused her to develop headaches of such lancinating pain, that servility became preferable to conflict.

Her deep blue eyes grew vacuous with staring; seeing not the scene before her, but those of childhood punishments; a strap flung across her buttocks; a slap across the face; sudden yanking of her hair; and once, of being pushed so hard she fell and struck her head on the oaken arm of a heavy chair. The scar above her left eyebrow was still visible. Yet, ever after, amid the memory of oozing blood and the over-excited distress of both parents, Rosina recalled most vividly her father's anguished cry. "… tut mir leid! sehr leid! sehr leid!" (so sorry, so sorry, so sorry)

But that was childhood and all so very long ago. He no longer dealt out bodily punishment. This was due in part to her being a head taller than he, but more specifically to her rarely giving him cause.

Why Rosina still existed in such a state of submission she could not have explained to anyone, much less to herself.

Yet she often vacillated into secret thoughts, believing, and even planning—fruitlessly—how someday the sinister veil which lay like a shroud around her heart would dissipate through some mysterious, external force and bring her radiant happiness.

Now she drew in her breath, letting it out with a deep sigh of resignation. The weighty notebook slipped and fell with a dull thud upon the floor. The pencil rolled errantly beneath the radiator and the clacking typewriters stopped their rhythmic beat.

Rosina felt all eyes focused upon her. Quickly, she stooped and retrieved the fallen articles. Flushed hot with embarrassment, she hurried the length of the room to the glass-enclosed office of her supervisor, Fraulein Bondt. With every step the staccato click of her heels beat hammer—loud inside her ears.

She knew that Jeanette Bondt had been watching her. Now looking at Jeanette's bright, blonde hair; the shrewd gleam in her golden eyes; and the benign indulgence in her smile, Rosina felt the suffused flush of her cheeks recede to normal.

"Come in." said Jeanette as she leaned back in her swivel-chair. "Do sit down and take the weight of the world off those pretty shoulders. Five minutes," admonished the older woman, in a tone more facetious than reprimanding, "… is a long time to be staring out of that window. Tell me, has a Maharaja arrived, or did someone fall off the flag-pole?"

Rosina laughed. The amusement, which divided her full lips, made deep crescents below her cheeks and ignited sparks in her dark blue eyes.

"I know I should have been working. But there I stood… day-dreaming again."

Jeanette cast a sweeping glance through the glass wall at her employees, who were again working like sixty automatons. Then, fixing her eyes on Rosina's slim form, the glow of youthful skin, and the shock of softly waving hair, she spoke with a plaintive air.

"Rosina. You are me, as I was thirty years ago. Young, restless, so damned vulnerable and… just as stupid!"

Rosina's intent gaze lowered at the word, stupid. Inadvertently her eyes studied the printed label of the notebook set squarely on her lap. Large black letters; COLONIAL POWER CO., melded one into another. She blinked, and fixed upon the smaller print below, Turbine-Generators. Her job was to translate the German text into English. Although unnerved by Jeanette's astute perception, she made no attempt to answer. As a matter of course she had to accept such criticism. For Jeanette was also cousin to Rosina's mother, and the only energizing spark in the life of the docile, spiritless girl.

To avoid further discussion, Rosina rose to her feet and spoke softly. "I must get to work on this. May I have Heddy to help me with it?.

"Certainly. It has to be finished by Friday afternoon. Ask whomever you need...."

Because Jeanette paused, Rosina knew intuitively that something more would be said.

"Your mother told me that you will be marrying Karl

Niederer... sometime soon. Have you decided exactly when?"

Rosina had almost reached the doorway. Her shoulders tensed, and without turning around, she answered, "No, I have not. Well... what I mean is, n... not right away." To herself, she thought, Oh my God! What a silly way to answer Jeanette. Quick tears stung her eyes. Then, with both arms hugging the notebook to her breast, she spun around.

"Jeanette, you know I cannot do it"

Fighting to control a flood of threatening tears, she looked to the older woman for understanding. "You know I do not want to marry Karl!"

"But father insists..." said Jeanette dourly, "so you delude yourself into thinking that someday... you will!"

"I do not want to hurt Vati or Mutti, and I do not want to hurt Karl. I do not want to hurt anyone!"

"Karl!" retorted Jeanette, "could do with some hurting!" The idea of mating you with him is like casting pearls before swine. But, since no one asks for, or would even listen to my opinion, it is better to keep my mouth shut!"

Her voice now rose in vehement anger. "Thirty years ago, I was—like you—the subservient daughter. Where has it left me? Alone… fifty-five years old and mothering a motley collection of foreign secretaries!" She moved her head slowly from side to side and interposed in dull monotone. "What we, as women, think and feel and want, makes absolutely no difference to fathers who think they own us… body and soul!"

Rosina sighed. "Mutti told me that you once had father-trouble, too."

"Mine was a bit different. Johann wants you to marry someone you do not love. My father refused to let me marry someone I loved… very much."

Rosina searched her cousin's face, then ventured to ask, "Your friend, the doctor?"

Jeanette's eyes flashed with amusement. "Did your mother tell you about that?"

"Only that you loved him a long time, that even after the war you saw him again, and that because of him, you never married."

"Which quite neatly sums up the life of Jeanette Bondt!" she said with dry sarcasm. "Tell me something. If you and Rosa have such frank discussions, what are her true feelings about your marrying Karl?"

"Mutti always agrees with Vati; with whatever he wants, whatever he demands! It seems that she even anticipates his thinking."

"I know that! But doesn't she ever talk to you about the personal things which are close to a woman's heart?"

This was a new thought for Rosina. She tried to visualize her mother as having any emotional thoughts of her own, so the answer she gave Jeanette was vague and vacuous.

"No, we hardly ever talk about… anything personal."

It was only with Jeanette that Rosina talked freely.

Now, thinking of the long engagement to Karl, and of the strange fact that he still wanted to marry her, she asked Jeanette if she too, did not think this odd.

"Ha" Jeanette responded with a toss of her head, her eyes wide with derision. "Not at all. It is really quite simple. He cannot get you into bed any <u>other</u> way."

Rosina shared her amusement. "You do say exactly what you think. And I suppose I asked for that. But seriously now, tell me what would you do in a situation like mine?"

"Me?" A wry smile crossed Jeanette's face. "I would probably go off somewhere, by myself, on a vacation. Why of course," she added with obvious delight. "That is precisely what you should do. After you finish that proposal, take a holiday. Get away from Zurich! Do something different... without your parents, and certainly without Karl!"

"But I do not have holiday until August!"

"Ach Himmel!" said Jeanette impatiently. "I am telling you that you need a vacation now! So, after you deliver that translation to Herr Lander, there is nothing else pressing. In fact, you could leave on Saturday."

"Wh... where...?" Rosina stuttered. "Where would I go?"

"Lugano would be best. At least the sun is shining there. The Beau Rivage is a good hotel, not too expensive. I am sure you would like it."

She moved her hand in abrupt dismissal. "Now, off with you. We both have work to do.

Chapter Two

After Rosina had gone, Jeanette turned her attention back to the papers on her desk, but the printed words conveyed no meaning. Beau Rivage, she mused, remembering it as one of her happier recollections. There were others; Walhalla in Saint Gallen, Simplon in Berne, des Alpes in Arosa. Ah yes, she remembered. For more than twenty years she had gone on so many holidays, sometimes with Wilhelm, sometimes alone.

She stared at blurred copy, seeing only a superimposed likeness of the man she loved. Useless admonition choked her whispered words. "I should have married him, even though Papa said, 'No!'"

In waves of reflection, she recalled Lugano during a family vacation in the summer of 1939. Feeling that all the world was hers for the reaching out—Jeanette sat on the beach beside another girl, providing, she thought hopefully, invitation for the two medical students from Germany. Thus, not unexpectedly, two shadows fell simultaneously upon the sand. A masculine voice spoke above her head.

"Peter and I, having a preference for blondes, came to the obvious conclusion that you two would undoubtedly have a similar interest in two, young, handsome men." As he said this, he dropped down beside her, while the other one lowered himself next to Katrin.

"Is that so?" Jeanette asked with keen interest, stretching her head to look past him. "Where do you suggest we look?"

"No further, Liebchen. I am called Willy and he is called Peter."

As she reminisced about that casual beginning, she saw, with her mind's eye a clear picture of the young man who had so captivated her heart. Thick dark hair, cropped short enough to stand up straight, twinkling blue eyes which would not be serious, and a perpetual grin around

his lips. When she stood up to him, she realized that he was not much taller than herself. But his manner, his regal bearing, and gay trivial banter, all served to convey an air of complete self-confidence.

He led her into a happy maelstrom from which she had no desire to be rescued. Even their moment of truth had been a haphazard incident. Returning from a dance, Willy said, "Let's cool off the tired feet." So they had slipped off shoes and stockings and waded into the cooling water of Lake Lugano.

He pulled her to him, kissing her mouth with intense passion. She felt a sharp contrast between her wet feet and the sensual delight of the warm embrace. And when he relaxed his iron grip, she stared at eyes she could not see, because bright moonlight shone into her own.

"That was pretty good," He laughed, and then repeated the performance. Then, breathing heavily, he said, "Liebchen, Liebchen, I am getting the idea that you might love me." And she, too overwhelmed to be coy, had smiled an answer, her gold-brown eyes alive with promise.

"Hey, you do!" he rejoiced. "And I do! Gott im Himmel, but this is marvelous!"

He released her to look away, at dark mountains across the lake. And she noticed that the self-assured Wilhelm Gottfried had, for the moment, lost his smile.

Hand in hand they waded ashore. She sat on a bench while he dried her feet with his handkerchief. She slipped on her stockings.

"After examinations next year, we will get married." It was a statement, requiring no answer. He put her shoes on her feet.

"But Willy?" she asked, searching his face while he brushed sand off his soles. "Don't doctors have to serve a longer time even <u>after</u> the examinations?"

He put his shoes on, then rubbed his hands to rid them of sand.

"Certainly, But my government encourages early marriage." He moved his hand to frame her chin. His free arm slipped across her back. "Especially…" he continued as his mischievous grin crept back in place, "… between young, brilliant men like me, to beautiful, healthy girls like you."

Another prolonged kiss prevented her from analyzing this statement as being any different from his usual mocking nonchalance.

Papa quietly observed the escapades, deeming it a summer romance which would pass away as do the autumn leaves. He concluded—illogically—that because he had no use for Germans, his daughter should be of the same mind.

Thus it came as an unbelievable shock when the young man came to Zürich the following spring to make known his most honorable intentions.

"Marry you!" Herr Bondt exploded. "My daughter marry a—a German!" He could have said python, so venomous was his tone. Rising anger brightened the color in his face. His eyes shrank to narrow slits. With hard-set jaw, he took a deep breath as hateful words spewed forth. "A horde of war fiends! That's what you are; arrogant, despotic tyrants! Ruled by a madman! Why I would rather see her <u>dead</u>, than married to a Nazi!… Heraus! heraus!" [heraus = out] He shouted loudly, "Get out of my house Never, not ever, shall you see Jeanette again!"

Thereafter, Papa kept her under strict surveillance, forcing her to drop her business school classes. She accepted the docility necessary to one who has neither money nor independence. Docile? Yes. But resigned? No! She planned imaginative escapes which never materialized.

Toward the last of August when Nazi rumblings presented daily assaults through every news-cast, Papa Bondt relaxed his vigilance and Jeanette returned to school. On her first day of freedom she telephoned Freiburg. Eager with excite- ment she breathed ecstatically, "Oh Willy,

Willy, it has been so long!" A thrill of pure joy permeated her whole body.

But the voice which answered purveyed no joy. "Jeanette, listen to me. Last week I…."

"Yes?"

"Last week I was married."

"Oh no, Willy! No" Her voice had a horrible sound.

An agonized sob caught in her throat. "No, Willy, no! Oh God, no! How… How could you?

"Jeanette, Jeanette, please,"- he begged. "Try to understand. Things are…." He paused, choosing his words carefully. "Our way of life is… a… different here…."

The attempted explanation was lost on the silenced, apathetic girl.

"Jeanette?" he asked, deep pain in his voice.

"Yes?" came the pathetic answer.

"I tried in many ways to reach you. Twice I went to Zürich. Once to your school, and another time I waited in vain across the street from your house. I had to tell you that, but there is something more important I must say. Your father was right. No Swiss girl should marry a…." His voice caught on the word, "Nazi". He could not even say it. His voice dropped to a pain filled whisper. "You see, my dearest Jeanette, I cannot even say, auf Wiedersehen, as I would wish, but rather… a sad adieu."

The following morning, September first, Hitler's legions struck Poland without warning and smote terror into the hearts of all mankind. Jeanette finished school and went to work for Siegwart Freres. She tried dating other men, but a vision of Wilhelm, trapped in a life not of his choosing, haunted every effort. The war droned on, feeding daily torment to the civilized world. In 1943 Jeanette's father died. Her mother sold their house and moved back to Wallisellen, into the ancestral home. Jeanette, twenty-three, moved into her own apartment.

One cold December evening in 1945, she answered a knock at the door and saw a stranger standing there. A thin, tired-looking stranger who reminded her of Willy.

The sudden, horrifying realization that it was indeed, Wilhelm Gottfried, seized her with frightening panic. She slapped both hands against her face. "O mein Gott. Mein Gott!" she gasped hoarsely, as she stepped back into the room, giving him indication to enter. "How?" she asked, her voice still rasp with incredulous wonder, "How did you find me?"

"The telephone book," he said, closing the door behind him.

He wore no boyish grin upon his face; no joyous sparkle in his eyes. She studied the blue depths so near her own two frightening mirrors which had seen too much of war; of blood; of suffering; and privation.

The encounter, long dreamed of by Wilhelm, but deemed utterly impossible by Jeanette, moved them both with desperate need. He gathered her into his arms and when his lips pressed hers, no further conversation was possible. Six years just melted away, as does snow in a quick spring thaw.

He covered her cheeks with kisses; her ear, her neck; and the place on her throat where her blouse opened. A tingling, warm sensation spread from her shoulders downward through her body.

Raging waves of desire, long subdued, flowed from one into the other, until it engulfed them both. And she, feeling as though tidal surf carried them as one being, kissed his forehead as he pressed his lips ever closer to her breast.

His passionate longing burst suddenly forth. "Ah, my Jeanette, how I love you. How I have wanted you, needed you... and only you!" He raised his head and whispered softly into her ear. "Liebling, I want to stay... all night... here with you."

She drew in her breath and pressed her cheek against his. "Yes, I know," she said, then took his hand and led him into the bedroom.

It is said that time heals all wounds. But Jeanette soon realized that salve alone does not heal a deep gash, that only stitches serve to bind the flesh. They continued to live, not only in separate countries, but in separate worlds. Willy in Freiburg with his wife and daughter Marlene. She, alone in Zurich; assuming increased work-responsibilities throughout the passing years. The high points of her existence became his occasional week-end visits; Sunday night phone calls; and twice-yearly resort-vacations; each one a new adventure spiked with danger and delight… until the last, in Arosa.

The factory whistle blasted her reverie. With a start, she realized that not a word on the papers before her had penetrated her consciousness. She watched the girls close their desks and cover typewriters. She heard their chatter—a monotone of many languages—as they left the floor by lift or stairs. Then silence. All but one had gone.

Jeanette's gaze followed Rosina, who moved gracefully across the outer room. The youthful figure wearing the jaunty red skirt, cut high above her knees, provoked a sudden realization that this lovely girl—who was all of the children whom she would never have—could not be allowed to waste her life as she had done. Rosina came closer and entered Jeanette's office.

"Anything I can help you with?" Rosina asked.

"No thanks. There is nothing here that cannot wait until morning. Right now, my prime concern is your getting away from Zürich."

"Oh that. Well yes, I have decided to take your advice, that is if I can work up enough courage to tell Vati."

"Oh Rosina! Stop being such a goose! You are thirty years old. When are you going to start making your own decisions?"

Rosina bent to lay an arm across Jeanette's shoulders, and said, I love you. You have more concern for me than anyone I know. So worry not. I will do this, I promise." Then, brushing a quick kiss upon the side of Jeanette's forehead she turned and hurried away.

Alone now, Jeanette stared vacantly across the empty room. Her thought wandered back to that last night in Arosa, five long months ago. What started out as a week of skiing, dancing, and cozy dinners, had been abruptly shortened by an incident which intruded upon their privacy.

That night as she lay in bed waiting, Willy walked aimlessly about the room, then finally stopped to gaze out of the window. Darkness shadowed the room, whose only light came from the bathroom to cast an oblique white shaft across the floor. The silhouette at the window stood remarkably still. She could not bear it.

"Willy?" she asked softly. "What is it? What is the matter?"

He turned around and strode across the room to the night table beside the bed. Picking up a cigarette pack, he drew one out and clicked a lighter. His face appeared like a bizarre mask in the flickering light.

He answered, in a painfully quiet voice.

"In the lobby, as we came through, were some people from Freiburg. The woman is a patient of mine, and a close friend of Henrietta's. She will undoubtedly tell her... and," he added with sour vehemence, "everyone else in Freiburg"

"And you are worried about it?"

"Not about Henrietta, certainly, but others?, Yes. Especially my daughter Marlene."

"It is quite simple," she had then suggested. "I will take the train back to Zürich in the morning, In a few days you can drive back. She reached for his hand. "Come to bed now and for tonight... let's not think about it."

Later, before he drifted off to sleep, he had murmured, "I love only you, Jeanette. I always will."

Now, in the stillness of her office—as she lived again in memory—tears forced their way between her eyelids, slid down her flushed cheeks, and dropped onto her folded arms. For the thousandth time, she recalled their early morning farewell, not then knowing that his whispered promise was but a glib fabrication from a half-awakened man. "Good-bye for now, my darling. In a few days, I will telephone."

But he had not done so. Not that week or the next. And now five months had passed. Five months of black agony. Five months of crying within, which was more debilitating than tears released. At times it seemed as though weeding—claws pulled wide her ribs and left a gaping canyon from throat to loin. For five months she had worked long hours; her only antidote for filling the bottomless void.

A sound at the door startled her. She looked up to see her managing director, Otto Lander, leaning casually against the frame of the office doorway. A bemused expression framed his light blue eyes. A black homburg perched at a ridiculous angle on the back of his once blond hair which had now turned silvery gray.

"You going to work all night?" he asked in a breezy tone.

His friendliness changed her mood abruptly. She dabbed a handkerchief across her eyes and stood up.

"No Otto, of course not. Some checking is… well, easier after the girls leave."

"You work too hard. Leave it. Come on, I will drive you home."

Chapter Three

On Friday afternoon, Otto Lander sat before his massive walnut desk, in the quiet inner sanctum of his office, protected from intruders by a receptionist outside the closed door. Now that door had opened and a beautiful girl entered, crossed the room, and laid two large volumes on the desk.

"I am Rosina Wyler," she said. He watched her lips as she spoke. They were warm and full. Her eyes were keen and direct. "This is the proposal, and a copy, for the United States company: Colonial Power." Not even the shadow of a smile appeared across the glowing cheeks.

"Let's have that over again," said Otto. "This time with a big smile."

"Wh... at?" she asked with astonishment.

"You are too pretty to be so sober," Otto continued. "I would like to see you smile.

Instantly her expression brightened expansively. The lips parted above straight white teeth and the blue of her eyes transformed into sparkling sapphires. The change even brought a lilting joy to her words.

"I always thought, Herr Lander, that you were some sort of unreachable ogre. But you're not. Not at all. You are...." She paused, and a slight flush heightened her cheeks.

"Go on," urged Otto, hoping to enjoy some gay repartee.

She lowered her eyes. "I started to say that... I thought you... rather charming."

"Thank you, my dear. That is better than your thinking I was a lecherous old man bent on seduction." He chuckled, then went on. "Actually, I have three daughters who are probably about your age, and though I also have one son, I'm quite partial to girls."

His tone changed to a more serious vein. "Thank you for delivering the proposal. I assume you are Fraulein Bondt's assistant?"

"Yes."

"She tells me that you are now going on holiday?" He was thinking of how lovingly Jeanette had spoken of this girl. "Where are you going, may I presume to ask?"

"To Lugano. That is what she… ah, what Fraulein Bondt suggested."

"Ja ja. Lovely place, Lugano. Well, Fraulein Rosina, it has been a delight to meet you. Have a good trip."

"Thank you." She nodded to him briefly, turned away and left the room, closing the door softly behind her.

Otto leaned back and locked his hands behind his head. For the moment, he had not the slightest interest in turbine generators. She thought I was "Charming," he mused. Perhaps, with a little encouragement, the lovely Jeanette might think so too. His thoughts turned to the evening, two days earlier, when he had taken her home.

As he had followed her toward the lift—about twenty-five steps—he had ample time to study her figure. He missed nothing; from the short blonde hair curling briefly at the nape, to straight, proud shoulders encased in a simple brown dress—which also neatly covered well-rounded hips. Beneath the hemline were a couple of shapely legs that moved with graceful, determined steps. She was, he thought, still youthful—filled out to luscious proportions – and… though the realization surprised him, rather desirable! Although he had worked closely with her for many years, for the first time, he saw her as a delectable female.

In the lift he glanced at her face and knew she had been crying. Why? What the hell had she been crying for? Another thought nagged him. Why had she never married?

Even after he had let her off at her apartment on Bergstrasse, and driven downhill toward the lake, the seeds of questioning nagged even more. He reflected on their conversation, with astute insight. When anyone chatters on so purposely about something irrelevant, such as she had about the girl, Rosina, it is mere subterfuge covering something far more vital. At the bottom of Ramistrasse, he turned left onto the quay and drove slowly along Bellerivestrasse to his home.

Inside the house, he had walked directly to the hall mirror, smoothed his hand across thin gray hair, studied the wrinkles around eyes and mouth, then patted the slight paunch at his waistline. He had laughed at the image there before him. "You damned fool. You're sixty years old!"

He had gone into the kitchen to see what the maid, Tina had left for his supper. He never wanted her to stay through the evening, not merely because she chattered on senselessly in Italian—little of which he understood—but because he actually wanted to be alone.

Later that night, as he drank his usual brandy, the vision of a form dressed in brown, refused to leave him. But even more haunting... was a damnable pretty face, the eyes of which—as she had thanked him for the ride—sparkled like gems of fiery topaz! With a trembling hand, he poured himself an extra shot. He had needed that, sorely needed that... if he was going to get any sleep.

The intercom buzzer pierced his reverie.

"Bitte?" he answered.

"Herr Lander, die Herren Fairbanks und Eaton von Colonial Power Company sind hier."

He bade her show them in. Then with beaming ebullience Otto arose from his chair and moved toward them, his hand thrust out like the prow of a ship. "Good afternoon, Gentlemen."

After vigorous hand-shaking, and a few questions about their three days of sightseeing, he turned off the effusive manner as easily as flicking a light switch. He motioned to chairs. "Please be seated."

Fairbanks, the elder of the two, slid his tall, slim body into one of the black leather chairs, while young Eaton wandered to the window. With both hands thrust into his pants pockets, the latter surveyed an inner court—completely flower-carpeted in expansive colors around a central fountain of cascading crystal shards.

Otto glanced at the young man's rugged shoulders beneath a head of thick blonde hair flowing in waves over the top of his collar. The contrast of feminine looking hair above such masculine shoulders seemed an absurd incongruity. "Today's youth!" he thought with disgust. "Why do they want to look like girls?"

He turned his attention to Fairbanks. The appraisal here suited him better; Sandy hair, neatly cut, sincere eyes, light blue, he thought, forty maybe. Ah yes, more sensible, this one.

He slapped his hand down upon one of the proposals lying on the desk, and said, "Now to business, eh?" We have completed our estimate for manufacture of the steam-turbines you want. You will find this complete with import duties, delivery dates, and other pertinent data which we discussed with you previously.

While he continued with more trivia regarding the proposal, he observed that the eyes of Fairbanks were studying a family photograph on the wall. It was an old picture of his wife and four children.

"My children...." Otto started to explain.

"You're a lucky man to have such a family," said Fairbanks urbanely, leaning sideways to see better.

"By that admission, I assume that you are... not married?"

"No, I'm not." It was said quietly. "But," he added with a wry laugh, "I have had my chances. Then, each time, either she broke it up... or I did."

"Ah, yes, well, don't wait too long. Life passes quickly. Those children are a case in point. Every one of them is now grown up and married. And my wife, Helene..." he hesitated, then swallowed hard. "She died a year ago October."

"Oh, I <u>am</u> sorry."

Lugano Holiday

The perfunctory apology had come so abruptly, Otto scarcely heard. He now noticed that Eaton's attention had been drawn to the photo, for this one had moved to observe that which was under discussion. "She certainly was a beautiful woman," said Eaton softly, with due respect in his voice.

A quiet, "yes," was all that Otto could manage. To hide the sudden heart-aching memory. he stood up and handed over

the proposal, which the American client casually slipped unopened, into a tan leather briefcase.

"You don't want to look it over". Otto asked with astonishment. "Perhaps you... ah... would have questions?"

"We'll look it over tonight at the hotel, then bring it back in the morning for you to air-mail to the States."

During this exchange, Otto watched the younger man wander around the room, stopping to glance briefly at one of his trophies; a mounted elk's head, then at his diploma from the Polytechnic University, and finally halting before one of his prized possessions: a Bochlin painting of a nude male figure beside a female form, mistily clad in diaphanous gauze.

Fairbanks had risen to his feet. "Did you remember, Mr. Lander, that late tomorrow morning, we travel to Lugano for a brief vacation before going home?"

"Ah, yes," beamed Otto. "Lovely place, Lugano. Sunny and warm."

Fairbanks persisted. "I wondered if you would arrange for a hotel there for us?"

"A hotel? In Lugano? Hmmn." He pursed his lips and thought about it. "No problem. It should take but a moment."

As he pushed a button on his private phone, he thought. "Lugano is where the pretty Rosina also goes. Hmmn."

The phone's response was instantaneous.

"Jeanette," said Otto. "Fur die zwei Amerikaner, kannst du ein Hotel in Lugano empfehlen?"

Virginia C. Taylor

The voice on the phone hesitated, then spoke decisively. "Ja Otto, das Beau Rivage."

Otto thanked her. He then told the men that his secretary would make the reservation. He wished them a pleasant vacation and ushered them out the door.

Then, with more self-satisfied complacency than he had for some time experienced, he returned to his chair, tilted it back, and placed all of his fingertips together, pressing the index set upon his lips. He began to speculate on which one of the Americans would most likely interest the pretty Rosina. His eyes rolled upward and a smirk of joy swept across his face. He chuckled, then mused to himself, "this old blood is not as tired as I thought. Why, life—even for me—might again become interesting." He closed his eyes and conjured up visions of Jeanette in more glamorous clothes than those she wore each day to the office. As he mentally dressed her in silky cerise, ruffled around her throat, then in black velvet, low-cut, shapely and divine, his breathing quickened. But his final fantasy which placed her in a sheer night-gown, perhaps of green, or maybe peach, caused his blood to run fast and hot.

As he consciously withdrew from the limbo of imagination, he suddenly realized that not all of his passion had died when he lost his beautiful Helene.

Chapter Four

On Saturday morning, an hour before her train's departure, Rosina sat in the car beside her father as he drove down into the city. It had been raining since early morning and torrential rivulets streamed down both sides of Leonhardstrasse. Turning sharply onto Weinbergstrasse into a glut of heavier traffic—and barely missing a collision with a blue streetcar—Johann tightened his jaw and swore beneath his breath.

Rosina felt his irritation deeply, well knowing that it was directed more at her than at the present situation. Ever since Wednesday evening when she had informed him of the impending trip, she had endured his wrath with placid stoicism. An inner compulsion, far stronger than his angry irrationality, had buoyed her spirit with indomitable courage. "Let him rant and rave," said the inner voice. "His words cannot hurt you."

She had intended taking the trolley to the station, but when the rainstorm worsened, Johann insisted on driving her there.

Now, approaching Central Plaza, the thrust into even greater traffic infuriated him further. Words whined through his grated teeth. "This is not proper at all! This going off by yourself!"

"Proper or not, Vati, I am doing it. I am going."

They were on Bahnhofbrucke now. Johann spoke fiercely. "You care about no one but yourself".

"Ha! Myself is it?" she retorted. "For almost thirty years I do things your way! Now that I do something my way, you call me selfish!"

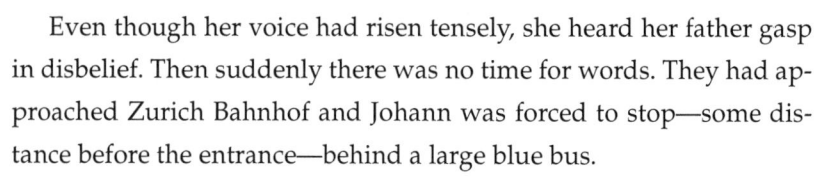

Even though her voice had risen tensely, she heard her father gasp in disbelief. Then suddenly there was no time for words. They had approached Zurich Bahnhof and Johann was forced to stop—some distance before the entrance—behind a large blue bus.

As Rosina leaned over and kissed his cheek, her lips felt his tightened jaw. A momentary pang of remorse stung her. Yet, she willfully opened the door, climbed out of the car and handed her suitcase onto the gray, wet, pavement. Swiftly, she slammed the door and cried out, "Auf Wiedersehen!" But the words were lost amid other noises of Bahnhofplatz.

Carrying her suitcase, she hurried toward the main doorway, entered, and disappeared into the flowing crowd inside.

Nearby, in the Swissair reservation office, Ward Fairbanks waited for Stanley Eaton. He had sent Stan out to Siegwart Company to return the proposal and to clarify some minor details. Having just confirmed their flight to the States for the following Saturday, he now stood at the window watching sheets of rain wash across the pavement. People scurried along the sidewalk holding umbrellas like shields against the wind. Some of them became swallowed by a descending stairway which would carry them beneath the busy plaza. Two boys, hatless, their jackets flying open, ran to catch a blue and white street-car. A number 6 on a panel along the roof designating its destination.

A taxi halted against the curb. Ward watched Stanley pay the driver, jump out, slam the door and run, all in one quick operation.

Together once again, the two men picked up their bags and followed the painted yellow line out to the track gates. The small hand on the concourse clock pointed to eleven. They paused before a board which read, Bahn-steig 2—Gotthard—Chiasso. Abfahrt 11:18.

Beside them stood a girl who also read the board. She wore an opaque raincoat which in no way concealed a bright yellow dress, so trimly fit it outlined the attractive shape of its wearer.

She turned away abruptly, walked through the gate and alongside the coaches until she found the one which said, Lugano. She knew by the sound of footfalls directly behind that the two men were following her. She climbed the steps, moved casually down the aisle and glanced into each compartment. On finding one occupied by only two women, she moved inside.

Rosina sensed that these two women would probably not trouble her very much. They were both extremely fat. She thought, irreverently, that they resembled over-stuffed laundry bags with short protuberant legs stuck onto the bottom, like those of Humpty Dumpty's.

"Guten Morgen," said Rosina, as she laid her suitcase on the opposite seat.

"Guten Morgen, Fraulein," answered the one closest to her. "Aber es ist nicht wirklich sehr gut. es regnet zu sehr." *

*trans. (But it is not really good, it is raining too hard.)

A broad grin had spread across her round face. While the other woman—beside the window—nodded repeatedly, displaying the wide grin of a simpleton.

"Ja," said Rosina. quickly averting her eyes from the pitiable one; so quickly, that she came face to face with a man who appeared instantly beside her. She looked into brown eyes in a youthful face.

"Hello," he said. His beaming grin seemed to her, almost as simple as the unfortunate woman seated beside the window. Behind him, she noticed another man, a tall one, who smiled not at all, but seemed to be merely following the other's lead.

In that instant, a whistle piped a weird, shrill cry, and the train began to move. Rosina tried to brace herself, but unwittingly the back of her knees came to the seat's edge and she sat down instead. This placed her on the corridor seat beside the fat lady.

Each man in turn lifted his bag onto the overhead rack. Then the one who had spoken, placed his hand on her suitcase and pointed questioningly toward the rack.

The sign language amused her. It occurred to her that if she kept to

German, she would not have to engage in conversation with them. Especially this one, whose expression reminded her of Little Red Riding Hood's wolf.

"Ja, bitte," she answered, with a nod of her head.

He then seated himself directly across from her, while the tall man said, "Excuse me," and moved over to the vacant window seat. She watched him cross his right leg over his left, and turn his attention through a rain-streamed pane at a watery panorama of large white houses. Ignoring them both, she slid back onto the seat, opened her handbag, and drew out a paperback book.

Her self-designated companion now pulled a pack of cigarettes from his pocket and leaned over to offer her one.

She looked up, and refused by shaking her head sideways.

As he then lit his cigarette, the reflected light in his eyes seemed to bore through her. She became annoyed, and began rifling the pages of the book, trying to pretend that he was not there. She decided that these two were Americans, who, she had been told, were as brazen as Germans.

A train conductor slid open the compartment door and asked for the tickets of each occupant. At sight of the smoking cigarette, his expression grew noticeably dour.

"Nicht raucher!" he sputtered, shaking his finger at the offender.

He rambled blithely on in German – pointing first at the cigarette and then at the NICHT-RAUCHER sign beneath the window.

The young man, being somewhat confused, dropped the cigarette and ground it out beneath his shoe. "Oh Kay, " he answered, raising his hand in a brief salute to authority, "I get the message."

Rosina, amused by the incident, waited until the conductor left, then broke her silence.

"You did not really get the message. He told you to go to a smoking compartment." As she talked, she kept her eyes down, looking only at his hands placed on each of his knees.

"Ah, you speak English," he said. "Who cares about a smoke. I'd much rather talk to you."

"I was only... trying to help. I prefer to read, thank you." She again focused her eyes on a page in her book.

He tried again. "Miss? ... a... Fraulein?"

She looked up directly into his eyes and without a smile, said patiently, "Yes."—in a tone so incisive she felt that it should stop him cold.

"Uh... forget it," he grumbled, shifting sideways on his seat. The averted position caused him to stare out through the glass door where only the lake of Zurich could be seen in the murky distance.

For a while the five people rode in silence, a silence broken only by the rhythmic sound of wheels directly underneath.

Rosina soon found that she could not concentrate on the printed page. She lived again the ride with her father, heard again the bitter words. She recalled too, her mother's eyes, tear-streaked from a farewell, which she had made as devastating as though Rosina was going to the far corners of the earth—never to return. She sighed inwardly with the untenable pain of it. Raising her eyes she looked to the window,

Because she rode backwards, to see out, meant looking past the profile of the other man. The rainstorm, having lessened in velocity, had changed to a fine mist. The variety of the undulating landscape seemed to command his full attention. She refocused on his hair, which, she noted was shapely cut with a trim side burn. Of a tawny hue, it curved in silken waves back from a high forehead. Despite his lean frame, the lines of his face had a fineness like that of Roman sculpture.

He must have noticed something unusual ahead, for he suddenly leaned closer to the glass. Then turning abruptly, he spoke excitedly to his companion.

"Hey Stan!..." And in that instant, his steel-blue eyes caught hers full upon him. His next words came out a trifle more prosaic. "... Stan, slide over here and look at this mountain."

For Rosina, the disconcerting gaze struck such wonderment, she felt her heart, blood and nerves touched as if by an unseen magic wand.

The fat lady smiled indulgently. explaining to Rosina that it was the Rigi mountain, the first of the Alps that he was seeing. The conversation droned on in German; Rosina listening to words which she hardly absorbed. The two men—oblivious to the foreign language—stood at the window, caught up in the enchantment of the landscape.

There was a three-minute stop at Zug, then the train picked up speed as it skirted the western side of a wooded mountain. Below, steep banks curved down sharply into a tiny azure lake.

On the opposite shore, barely discernible in the brooding mist, a small village nestled in a bosom of verdant mounds. Immediately southward, the pyramidal Rigi dominated the entire scene. As the train moved ever closer, the mountain—by misleading phenomenon—moved further away.

Abruptly, the train entered a tunnel, which cut off the spectacular view. Lights came on. The tall man sat down. And the one called Stan left the compartment in search of a smoker.

The fat lady and the simpleton prepared themselves for leaving at the next station. Yet, neither stood until the train had completely stopped.

Rosina reached out to help them with their looped-string shopping bags, but the man moved more quickly.

"Here, let me carry those for her," he said, freeing them from Rosina's grasp.

"Oh! All right, " she said, relinquishing the bags.

The lady thanked Rosina. The simple one nodded profusely.

They waddled into the corridor. And the man—like a hired porter—followed doggedly behind.

While he was gone, she removed her coat and seated herself beside the window. When he returned he sat down on the opposite side.

"That was nice of you," she said, looking directly into his eyes. "

"Could you possibly think I would sit here and let <u>you</u> do it?" he asked. The smile he gave her softened his angular face. And the deep timbre of his voice was smooth and sensual.

To maintain a calmness—which had just been ruffled—she went on to explain. "They are mother and daughter. The simple-minded one is the result of measles during the mother's pregnancy. Life is... sort of difficult for the mother...."

"So they eat their way into oblivion?"

She considered this. "It does make one realize that what we think are great problems in our own lives are truly...." She searched for the English word which would clarify her thought.

"Unimportant?" he suggested.

"Yes, quite unimportant...."

The train moved, jerked a little, shunted backward, then stopped with a jolt.

Seeing his astonished frown, she explained. "We are being connected with another train which came down from Basel.

I remember this from a time when I was thirteen. I recall being very excited about everything along this rail-line."

Although his eyes sparked with interest, it seemed to her that he did not listen but intently studied the depths of her own. As she became acutely conscious of this penetrating stare, Rosina stopped talking. For a brief moment, each held the other's gaze; soft and transcendental.

She swallowed something intangible which had formed in her throat. Then she looked away and stared hard at the Arth-Goldau station sign.

The whistle piped. The train moved rapidly on its way.

"I think it's exciting," he said, picking up the thread of conversation. "And I'm a lot older than thirteen."

Her intent expression changed to one of amusement.

"Obviously, this is your first trip through the Saint Gotthard?" she asked, keeping her eyes on the passing landscape.

"Not only that. This is my first trip to Switzerland."

"You are American, aren't you?"

"Is it that obvious?"

Rosina laughed. "What else have you seen of our country?"

"On Wednesday we went to Sulzer Company in Winterthur. Then on to Saint Gallen where we stayed overnight. The next day we rode up the Säntis mountain in a cable car. In the afternoon we drove along the lake of Constance to a quaint village called Stein am Rhein. We spent Thursday night there and came back to Zurich through Schaffhausen."

"By yourselves?" she asked in a tone of disbelief.

"Oh no. Siegwart Company loaned us a car and a chauffeur."

She turned abruptly to face him directly.

"Siegwart Freres?"

"The same. "

"Are you and he…" she pointed a hand toward where his absent companion had gone. "Are you from Colonial Power Company?"

"Sure. But… how do you know about that?"

"I work for Siegwart. I am the one who… put the proposal together."

"You? You put all that together?" He stared at her with a benumbed expression, which conveyed more than a passing interest in that kind of ability.

"I… hope it was all right," she faltered. "I… only did the translating, and most of the typing. Other persons did the figures, and of course, the drawings."

"It was perfectly clear," he calmly assured her. Then to clarify his position further he explained.

"I am an electrical engineer and Stan is a whiz at mathematics. Between us we figure things out."

She assumed that to be a modest appraisal of their capabilities. It became clear to her why a man of such caliber as this one—quiet, well-mannered, and quite charming—consorted with a boorish plebeian like his companion. It also precluded her ideas of avoiding them. The contract with Siegwart Freres was too important to have her spoil it by being either rude or indifferent.

Lugano Holiday

Suddenly curious about their destination, she asked, "Now where are you going?"

"To Lugano. We were told that it's a beautiful spot for a vacation. Tell me, have you ever been there?"

"No," she answered gravely, reflecting on the odd coincidence that she was also going to Lugano, at this particular time, on this particular train. She looked down at her tightly clasped hands. "That time I made the trip with my parents, we went to Locarno."

The train pulled into another station. A large sign appeared directly before them. He read it aloud.

"Altdorf. Isn't this where William Tell supposedly shot his arrow?"

"Yes. But it is not supposedly. We believe it."

"Why not?"

Leaving Altdorf the scenery commanded attention. So they stood—faces against the window—watching it pass. Below, a wild unruly river plunged beneath a bridge to join another, the foaming Reuss. Looking upward, he pointed out a church tower and crumbling castle ruins showing through the mist. Underneath, bold precipices jutted confluently from the mountain's side.

The valley narrowed with the train's ascent, and away below to the south lay what seemed like a toy village and toy power station.

"That is Amsteg," she said matter-of-factly. "One of the stations which generates power for this line."

She sensed that he turned and looked down at the top of her head, for he was easily six or eight inches taller.

"There are not many people, I dare say, who know things like that" he said.

"Just where, except Siegwart's, do you think they get their equipment?"

"Of course. That's completely logical. Have you worked for them a long time?"

"Oh yes," she answered, and her voice was almost a sigh.

Virginia C. Taylor   37

"A long, long time."

She continued watching the rapidly changing diorama, staring vacuously, as though she glimpsed the past years; with the dull repetition in those ahead. Then suddenly, beneath them, a rushing, foaming river cut through a deep ravine, forming torrentious waterfalls. It hurled hard blocks of snowy ice in mad abandon through the gorge. Its roaring tumult could be heard even above the rhythmic clack of the train. In the excitement of it, her shoulder touched his arm. She felt the muscle hard beneath his jacket sleeve. A most unusual sensation pulsated through her; something strange and uncontrollable. Another bridge Another gorge! This one filled to the top with rising crystal mist. Her heart began to pound. The water whirled around. Was it tossing her with the same unmerciful force as the ice cakes, pummeling through the gorge toward a distant, unknown abyss?

The train entered a tunnel. An abrupt move which helped her to regain equilibrium. Greatly disturbed, she sat down. Had he, she wondered felt any of the same sensation? She dared not look up. Instead, with a trembling hand, she reached for her book and opened it, unaware that it was

upside down.

"What is your name?" he asked.

"Rosina Wyler," she answered, feeling a flush of blood heightening in her cheeks.

"Mine, " He reached over to right the book. "... is Fairbanks, Ward Fairbanks."

At that moment Stanley returned—swaying on unsteady feet—as the train, groaning and screeching, negotiated an inside curve. Without explaining her connection with Siegwart Company, Ward introduced Rosina to Stan.

All three, now became fascinated by the train's new direction, observing its sharp angle—coursing ever inward, snake-like through a dimly lighted tunnel.

The 'snake' soon emerged from the darkness, uncoiled itself to speed along new heights, hugging the mountains' sides so as not to tumble down into the Reuss Valley.

To orient themselves in this new location, they left the compartment and moved into the corridor. A hundred feet directly below, lay the tracks over which they had just traversed.

"A complete circle inside a mountain in less than three minutes," commented Stan. "Clever, these Swiss."

"I'll agree with that!" said Ward, admiringly. "Which, I might add, encompasses not only the Swiss collectively, but one small Swiss in particular."

To this Rosina bit her lip, but gave no response. His mood was light. Hers should be too.

There were two more loop tunnels, but the first made the most remarkable impression. In between lay such a unique display of church and village, of viaduct and transmission towers, of orange-roofed houses scattered across green country-side, amid curving gray roads, that it would defy miniature-railroad buffs to attempt an imitation.

Two girls stood on a geranium-bedecked balcony, watching the nine-car train—being both pulled and pushed by two electric engines—pass in review. The girls waved. Passengers waved back. The engineer piped the weird, plaintive whistle and the train sped southward, then northward, then south again, on its way to Göschenen.

More passengers came aboard at Göschenen. The coaches filled. Ward and Stan went to the dining car for lunch. Because Rosina had bought a sandwich and fruit from the kiosk in the Zürich station, she declined an invitation to join them.

Later, when the train emerged from the nine-mile Saint Gotthard tunnel, the sun shone bright, hot and dazzling, upon the blue and silver engine which slid to a graceful stop at the first town in the Leventina Valley: Airolo.

In mid-afternoon the train arrived in Lugano, disgorged several passengers, swallowed up a few others, then piped itself off to Chiasso and… eventually on to Milan.

While they were still on the train, Rosina had told Ward and Stanley that her destination was also Lugano. But not until the moment when all three entered the limousine sent up from the Beau Rivage, did they learn of being booked into the same hotel.

It was, therefore, a profoundly thoughtful trio who rode a silent mile—coursing downhill through narrow streets and along the lakeside boulevard—to Paradiso, on the western shore of beautiful Lake Lugano.

Chapter Five

Rosina's first glimpse of an extremely modern hotel whose six decks were intricately ribboned with blue plastic above a sweeping, curved marquee—belied Jeanette's description of a quaint Spanish style with tiny railed balconies. "I know it has been remodeled," Jeanette had said....

Now, with an awe akin to panic, Rosina viewed this ultramodern transition. She was prepared for quaintness... <u>not</u> for blue ribbons which seemed to flutter boldly, as with some brazen threat. Like the balconies which had been torn away and replaced, she felt stripped of her own prosaic past by this sudden thrust into modernity.

Not until she was taken to a third-floor room, where glass doors opened onto one of those cerulean balconies, and she looked out upon a calm lake and stalwart mountain, did a sense of time eternal bring her back to more rational substance. A substance whose solidity lasted only long enough for her to look about the room, then open her suitcase, and hang dresses on hangars in the wardrobe.

Then, a sudden disturbance.

The new sound came from a jangling phone. Hesitantly, she placed her hand on the receiver. Vibration from a second ringing surged through her arm and into a racing heart. "Rosina Wyler here," she answered calmly.

"Rosina, this is Ward. Stan and I are going swimming. Will you join us?"

Her breath caught. "N-no thank you," she said, then added quickly, "That is… not right now."

"All right," he said, deflation in his tone. "But, if you change your mind," he spoke hopefully, "Do come… please."

She replaced the receiver, kicked off her shoes, and dropped backward on the bed. By lying perfectly still, the pounding of her heart gradually decreased its intensity. One disturbing element that lingered was the disappointment in his voice; the other, a softly spoken, "please".

Thrusting her left arm upward, she read her watch: three-fifteen. Then, with both hands interlaced beneath her head, she stared at the ceiling. Like shuffled cards, the day's events cascaded through her mind. She saw her mother wailing in incomprehension, over <u>how her little girl could possibly go away all by herself</u>! And her father's tirades, his angry, senseless reprimands. She felt again, the train's rhythmic beat, heard its weird whistle, saw the countryside's rapid shift of scenery. And… the two American men—each one the antithesis of the other. Yet, the predominant impression was a frightening awareness that the stranger had set off an emotional response within her. Like flipping an electric switch, power had surged through her the moment his eyes held hers. Although she had turned away, the image held fast within her mind's eye. She visioned his sandy hair combed back to form a sweeping wave away from her forehead; his face, long and angular; his body, slim and graceful; his hands, moving with certainty when he had righted her book, and finally, the startling transmission from his eyes, a lighter blue than her own, with intensely deep black pupils.

Her eyelids closed as drowsiness veiled this deduction. She slept soundly—the dreamless sleep of exhaustion—then awoke suddenly with the split-second shock of being in a strange place. Drawing cramped arms from beneath her head, she sat up quickly, yawning as she rubbed her aching arms, and stood upon her feet. She straightened the yellow dress which had twisted around her hips and looked out at the azure lake, which sparked an idea, (quite original, of course) that swimming would certainly refresh her.

She passed a turquoise colored pool which contained many children splashing and shrieking with delight. She continued onward, down several steps to a dock at the lake's edge. She pulled on a white cap, tucking thick brown hair underneath the rubber over her ears and nape.

Out on the lake, yellow sails on a white hull flapped lazily, then filled with air as the boat skirted slowly away. Off to the right, several heads and occasional arms broke the waters surface. Out on a float, three persons lay baking in late-afternoon sunshine. On the dock beside her, an assortment of bikini-clad bodies and trunked torsos milled about. A transistor thumped a groovy beat. And more than one pair of male eyes riveted on the sprightly form encased in a mailot suit, the color of heavy cream.

She dived in, cutting neat and shallow beneath the surface, to emerge from the glide, several yards away. Using long, strong strokes, she swam out to the off-shore float where the three prone figures watched her approach: Ward, Stanley, and a girl with long flowing blonde hair.

"Welcome aboard, mermaid," said Ward, rising up on his knees.

Rosina had grasped the metal ladder and sprung like a water-sprite up onto the float's yellow deck. Shifting her legs over the rim, she positioned herself, allowing her feet to dangle over the edge.

"I'm glad you changed your mind," said Ward, dropping down beside her. His eyes sparkled delightedly, setting off a wide grin across his lean face.

"One cannot long resist… the lure of water," she said, still breathing deeply.

He introduced the blonde—a darkly tanned girl in a red bikini. "This is Bergit."

"Bergit Verlinde," she supplied gaily, "from Ultrecht." Sitting with both legs off to one side, the Dutch girl supported her weight on her left palm, reaching out the other to clasp Rosina's hand, then added warmly, "I am pleased to know you."

"Thank you. Are you also staying at Beau Rivage, or…" Rosina shifted her gaze to the nearby window-walled hotel, upon whose roof protruded four large letters, "… the Eden?"

"At Beau Rivage, with my mother, my father, <u>and</u> my brat of a sister Johanna," then added with an air of disgust, "She is twelve!"

The remark troubled Rosina, yet she responded with a knowing smile. Beside her Ward was appraising his reddened arms.

"I guess I have had enough sun for one day," he said. Turning to face her, he asked, "Will you swim with me?"

Without answering, she brought her feet up to a standing position and dived in. He followed. They swam—like two otters hardly breaking the surface—a hundred yards along the shoreline before Rosina turned back toward the shore.

Coming in shallow, they waded ashore. Rosina, pulling off her cap and loosening the wet ends of her hair while she walked across the sand. On the terrace, where she had left her things, Ward held up her orange-colored beach coat into which she slipped her arms. As she bent her head, using towel-encased hands to dry a mass of thick brown hair, he said.

"That cap doesn't keep your hair very dry."

"It is practically impossible when I swim and dive."

"Which, I observed, you do to perfection."

"Why, thank You," she said, smiling up at him. I love to swim." Suddenly self-conscious, she focused on the distant float where Stanley and Bergit still lay. Her voice became sober and strained. "If I were lucky enough to have a sister. I would not call her a brat."

"I dare say, you probably would not. But younger children are quite often a nuisance. I imagine that Bergit is about eighteen and finds the present age difference deplorable. I know, because my two sisters, six and eight years older than I, considered me a brat when they were in their late teens." He altered his voice to one of more pertinency and asked, "Do you have brothers, or are you an only child?"

"An only child of elderly parents." She said it softly, with an air of sad resignation. "My mother was forty, and my father forty-six, when I was born." Averting her face, she looked out across the lake to a cleft between two mountains. "I am all they have. And though I love them dearly, there are times which are… well… quite difficult."

Realizing that she had said too much to a stranger, Rosina stooped to put on her sandals and spoke abruptly, "If you will excuse me now, I will go in to change."

She knew, that because of her sudden rejection, he would not follow. Yet, as she walked across the gray flagstones, stopping momentarily at the street, then crossing onto the hotel's driveway, she was acutely aware that his eyes had done exactly that.

That evening, Rosina came down late for dinner. As she entered the dining area, a waiter approached, spoke briefly, then led her toward a small table. She wore a light green dress which floated casually above her knees as she followed him. The Dutch girl, Bergit, seated with her family, spoke to her as she passed, which Rosina politely acknowledged.

Now as she sat alone beside a large window, the dusky light from outside defined her profile. Beneath her high forehead, dark lashes swept against the rosy freshness of her cheeks. The aquiline nose, above full lips rouged in light orange, accented the thrust of chin, which held its own set determination. If she seemed at ease, it was because that determination acted to placate an inner turmoil—an inexplicable uncertainty of not knowing quite how to handle herself if, for instance, the Americans were seated elsewhere in the room. Amid the muffled sounds of voices and of laughter, were they watching? Perhaps too… even discussing her?

During the interminable minutes she must wait for the waiter to bring her dinner, she turned to look across the lake at golden glints on the houses of Monte Brè, as layer by layer their glow diminished in the final rays of sunset. The diffusion also took the warmth from within her heart causing a bleak and sudden chill.

Then, simultaneously with the serving of dinner, lights came on in the room and Rosina's mood of self-preoccupation vanished.

When she had finished eating, she walked back across the lobby toward the lift. Blocking the way, as if by design, stood Stanley, Bergit, and Ward. The latter shifted himself to stay her advance. And as he looked down at her, she saw color rise in his face. His words came quickly, as though rehearsed.

"We are going to a cabaret where there is dancing and a floor show. Will you come with us?" His eyes searched hers with steady deliberation.

She swallowed, finding it hard to voice a refusal. Then finally she answered in a low voice. "Thank you, but no, it is best that I... not do so."

"Best for whom?" he asked pointedly.

"Best for all concerned," she said, looking down at his shoes of burnished cordovan. "I'm sure," she continued, "that you can find someone else who would be more... well... more fun, than me."

"If that's your criteria for not going, I don't accept it!"

She looked up in surprise, studied his eyes for a second, then glanced sideways at Stanley and Bergit, who standing shoulder to shoulder, holding hands, were smiling at each another. Tears threated her eyelids. Why shouldn't she go? Wasn't this why she had come? To do things she had never done before? To dare be a part of living... as others lived? She turned back and a brave smile formed around her lips.

"All right. Yes, I would like to go." Her bravado caused color to rise in her cheeks. To stabilize herself, she added with practicality, "I should perhaps, go up and get a sweater."

Even before the foursome entered the basement cabaret, the band's music sallied forth upon the night air. As soon as they stepped inside the two couples were directed to a table near the rear. Dreamy, waltz strains guided couples who danced in a clear area near the stage—the only brightness in the dimly-lit, smoky haze. The four were seated just as the languid music faded with a few mellow bars. Then, with a sudden assault upon the ears, the tempo changed briskly into a thumping, radical beat. Psychedelic lights swept across the floor. Musical potpourri hammered the room with a raucous, incessant din.

"Come on bay-bee!" Stanley urged Bergit, rhythmically moving his head and both hands to the surging tempo. Then pulling her by the hand, he led her off where they quickly merged into the group of variegated gyrating puppets.

"I am not very good at that," Ward said, adding by way of apology, "in fact, I have no intention of even trying it."

"It is rather exhausting," she said. Her eyes stared fixedly on the dancers to avoid Ward's direct gaze. Then, as though he sensed this in her, he began to explain.

"This sort of thing fits Stanley's age group better than mine. You see, I am forty, which is more than ten years older than Stan. When I learned to dance, it was <u>with</u> a girl, not at her."

Rosina laughed—a delighted chuckle, which eased her tension. She turned, looking up into his face, and in that moment, decided to be less serious. Bravely, and keeping her voice even, she ventured to comment, "The way your hair is cut short, and back off your forehead, in contrast to Stanley's indicates one difference in your ages." There were other differences, but she would let those pass.

"Which do you like better?"

"You are putting me on a spot," she parried.

"Uh, huh, <u>and</u> I'm waiting for the answer."

"I like… a neat haircut better." Her slightly parted lips enunciating the t sound, showed the even lines of her teeth gleaming white beneath the rosy fullness. Inadvertently she moistened them with her tongue.

An Italian waiter appeared and took their order for drinks. Rosina, who had never drunk anything but wine and beer, ordered a scotch and soda. Ward followed suit.

The music had faded away. Stan and Bergit now approached the table. Catching the waiter, Stan turned to Bergit,

"Name your poison, Blondie,"

"Cognac and water," she said, seating herself beside Rosina.

"I'll try anything," said Stan, turning to the waiter. "Make that two." He pushed his chair close beside Bergit's, put an arm around her waist and nuzzled his nose between the long golden strands to kiss her neck. She giggled and tried to bite his ear.

Rosina's hands—clasped beneath the table—tightened.

Instinctively, she felt her own age difference, her prudish restraint, her inability to relax into such abandonment. She wished she had not noticed their behavior, or… at least, not reacted visibly.

Bergit, sensing Rosina's disapproval, drew away from Stanley and turned to ask her where she lived and what she did.

I live in Zürich, and work in the correspondence department of Siegwart Freres.

Stanley, raising an eyebrow at this revelation, shot a quizzical look at Ward, who merely leaned back in his chair appraising each girl as they talked.

Bergit continued, "That is why you speak such good English. Are you wondering how I speak it so easily?" The latter, being more statement than question, she went on with the answer. "Two years ago I was an exchange student in the United States. Oh wow, was it great! When I get back to Ultrecht I'm going to work for American Express."

"Sounds more exciting than my job," Rosina commented. Mock envy tinged her voice,

Drinks arrived just as the music started up—this time soft and mellow. Rosina, feeling dry and thirsty, swallowed a large mouthful. Shocked by the bitter, ice cold bubble in her chest, she gasped and set the glass down hard upon the table.

"This music," he said, "is more to my style. Shall we dance?"

She rose to her feet, her heart hammering within her, as she walked ahead of him, to thread her way onto the dance floor. Then, pointedly avoiding his eyes, she placed one hand upon his shoulder and laid the other in his palm as naturally as though it were the twentieth… instead of the first time.

He guided her with easy grace in perfect coordination of his feet and hers. When he tightened his grasp against her palm, the increased pressure sent a current of energy coursing through her blood. And his gradually drawing her closer, filled her with surprised wonder whenever her body—ever so lightly—occasionally touched his. But most disconcerting were the lyrics of the music, which lent its own peculiar enchantment. "… they, like me… want to be… close to you." Despite the disturbing situation—which she did not really want to encompass her—she did control the agitation with remarkable poise.

"Do you know the words to this?" he whispered above her ear.

"Um humn," she murmured, for words… any words, were in that moment, impossible to speak.

They danced as one, oblivious of everyone and everything except, it seemed… each other.

Then all too soon, reality abruptly imposed itself. The music had finished, but he still held her close for those few seconds which passed until the music would continue. With an ever-so-light motion, she felt his lips brush the top of her forehead, and in that instant the music resumed.

Enveloped this time in waltz tempo, they danced in sweeping rhythm. A spirit of levitation seemed to lift her magically onto a floor of springy white clouds. In a timeless moment of ecstasy, the sheer green dress—long and diaphanous—floated in sensual swirls around her body. She imagined being raised; a ballet-dancer, high up on a strong male arm; then lowered, curving backward in a graceful arc, like a long blade of grass bending in the wind. Yet, with perfect coordination the whirling continued as, together, they turned and returned. And all of the time, fantasy and reality interwove, like warp and woof, shuttling back and forth, in and out, until each thread became part of a whole.

With a sudden flutter of notes, the music drew to a close, and Rosina opened her eyes. The unprecedented sensation of suspended time left her with hollow legs. Her arms had become two boneless limbs and her face was highly flushed. Ward's right arm still held her. With his free hand, he lifted her chin. "You know something?" he said with a rapturous smile, "You are really great!"

The compliment sparked a quick pulse beat in her throat. Then, a sudden fanfare tremolo signaled the beginning of a floor show. Together they threaded between the tables back to their own.

The murmur of voices and scraping of chairs hushed in anticipation. Beside the piano, a vocalist appeared inside a lighted circle. Wearing a skin-tight, blue satin gown, she purred through a rendition of "Les Bicyclettes de Belize"—first in French, then in English. When she had finished, the half-interested audience doled out metered applause.

With an instant hush and a vibrant roll of drums, all attention focused on the next performer, who spiraled out in a whirl of silver. She stopped for a quick bow, then straightened, throwing her silver-braceleted arms high above her head, revealing her entire costume for several seconds, before gliding into an adagio revue of classic beauty.

The costume, or rather, the lack of it, stabbed through Rosina's sense of propriety. A silver star barely covered the nipple of each breast; and a silver triangle; the juncture of body to legs. A narrow band around the hips supported a skirt of transparent net. Entirely open in front, the skirt carried a wide silver hem which dipped and whirled in sensuous undulation around the dancer's sinuous movements. Plaintive and eerie wailed the music, loud and stirring, beat the drums.

In shame-filled fascination, Rosina sipped her drink to alleviate a hot flush of embarrassment. Riveting her direction upon the dancer, she glanced occasionally at Ward, who divided his attention between herself and the performer. To her left, the faces of the other two glowed with animation.

At the finish—like a circumgyratory top finally run down—the flesh and silver figure lowered herself to form a compact cocoon. With bowed head, her long black hair streamed forward amid the silver band spread in a large circle around her on the floor.

Applause, spontaneous and long, displayed its own appreciation for the talented girl. Rosina clapped as loudly as the rest, for not to do so would have been rude... even boorish.

When the next act, a quartet of bearded, gyrating weirdoes came out thumping, beating and twanging, Ward asked if she wanted to leave.

"Oh, yes," she responded, her heart warm with gratitude.

He told Stan to take care of the check. They excused themselves and left.

Crossing the street, they walked back along the quay. His arm circled her shoulder—the hand placed lightly on her white cashmere sweater. Up ahead, loomed black-velveted Monte San Salvatore—like a brooding giant, stark and bold against the cerulescent sky. A garland of yellow lights streamed from summit to base and around that base, defining its juncture with the lake. Reflecting hotel lights threw jagged, yellow shafts into the mediterranean-blue-surfaced mirror of the lake.

They were both so deeply immersed in the dark, quiet beauty, their arrival at the flag-stone walk which led to the hotel, came with unwelcome abruptness. Ward stopped beside a red, wooden bench. "Let's sit here," he suggested. "It is too lovely to go inside."

Smoothing her green skirt beneath her, she sat down—the bench startlingly cool against the back of her legs. He moved close beside her, replacing his arm across her shoulders.

"It is lovely here," she said, thinking of the noisy cabaret with its constant motion—compared with this new serenity stretching in every direction. She drew in her breath. "I think this is the most exquisite place I have ever seen."

"You can say that again," he agreed.

Unfamiliar with the American expression, she turned to him with a questioning frown. Had she made an error in translation?

"The word, exquisite? It is not right?" she asked.

"It is very much right. No one could use a better word."

His fingers had begun to play with the loose brown hair on the back of her neck. She turned, and looked into his eyes in wonder,

"Exquisite describes more than the scenery," he whispered as he bent his head and kissed her briefly on the lips.

"Oh!" she said, lowering her face so that another light kiss found only her forehead. Her trembling hands lay one over the other in her lap and quickened blood went surging through her heart.

"Please don't kiss me again," she said in a quiet whisper.

"I'll apologize, but I am not sorry," he said ruefully, and pulled her head against his shoulder. His hand was strong and comforting upon her head; the touch so sure and gentle, her inner quivering slowly diminished and she became more conscious of the night's sounds; a quiet lapping of the lake upon the beach, muffled tires revolving along the boulevard, and distant music wafting subdued and mellow from the Eden hotel.

Chapter Six A

Later, from the hotel's balconies, the man from his, and the girl from hers, looked out at the back of the vacant red settee partly obscured by shrubbery. Each one visualized two heads silhouetted in the moonlight.

After a few minutes, Rosina moved away and made ready for bed. Ward remained seated at his viewpoint—smoking his pipe in contemplative silence until Stan came in at one o'clock.

"You missed all the fun, man, " beamed Stanley, throwing off his clothes in careless abandon. "What a place! What a doll!" Down now to his shorts, he came to the balcony doorway.

"That chick, Rosina, what's her hang-up?"

"I'm not sure, but it has something to do with the way she was brought up. For instance, her parents are old enough to be her grandparents and she is an only child."

"With that figure, she is no child!" He rolled his eyes suggestively. "I'll bet she is younger than I am, though she acts like she was… fifty!"

Ward drew on his pipe, blowing out smoke in a long wispy cloud. "I did not ask her age. It doesn't really matter."

"That's for sure," decided Stanley. "There are other girls around here."

"I'm sure there are," answered Ward in a non-committal tone.

"You'll find one tomorrow," Stan said as he turned away from the immobile figure leaning back in his chair, "who'll be a lot more fun, I'll bet."

"No," Ward contradicted, as his eyes looked down at the red bench. "Not tomorrow, or next week, or next year," he paused, "…because I am in love with this one."

"You're what!"

"You heard me."

"I heard you, but I don't believe what I heard."

"I believe it. Now I have to, … get used to the idea."

"Be my guest," quipped a bemused Stanley. He turned away in search of pajama pants. "Me, I'm going to bed."

"Good night."

"G'night."

"By the way…" added Stanley, with what he hoped was a casual afterthought, "Will you be out with her, tomorrow night?"

"I hope so."

Ward had stepped back into the room. He glanced at the half-naked Stanley, lying on his back, both arms thrust under his head.

"Do me a favor, and not come… in here… 'til after midnight."

Ward smothered an amused chuckle. "Damn sure of yourself, aren't you?"

"Oh man! I got reason to be. What a doll!"

"Pleasant dreams," taunted Ward.

"Oh hell!" retorted Stan. He rolled over and pulled the sheet over his head.

Awakened by sunlight warm upon her cheek, Rosina rose quickly from bed and faced the balcony. She stretched her arms luxuriously ceiling-ward while the sun shone through filmy pink pajamas. In wondrous fascination she moved to the sliding door, placed her hand on its frame and surveyed the mountains.

Spread before her, a sweeping mass of peaks loomed against a hazy sky. At left, barely visible, glowed one snow-capped cone. In the center, a double pinnacle—bereft of houses, except for its low left hip—gave precedence to a perfect green gem in the foreground: Monte Brè, upon which nestled a tiny church glistening through the morning haze. Lowering her gaze to the lake, through feathered palm-fronds, her eyes sought the red settee. In the clear light of day she wondered why she had allowed a stranger to kiss her.

Could it be that she had <u>wanted</u> to be with him… <u>wanted</u> him to touch her… and <u>wanted</u> him to kiss her? Oh! she groaned. "What happened to me? I did not come here to trifle with a stranger… an American! Liebe Gott! What would Vati say?"

The blood in her arms ran cold at the thought of her father and his punishments. She recalled vividly, at the age of four, how she had punched her finger into each one of a dozen perfect tomatoes, so he would be unable to… <u>always take the best ones to market</u>. The sting of his razor-strap, first on her buttocks, then on the back of her legs as she ran from him, allayed other incidents of being such a bad girl! That is, until a time when she was seven and had not returned immediately from school, but dallied at a friend's until nearly six o'clock! Besides the inevitable strapping, there had been a directive to bed—<u>without supper</u>! Ever since, she had been good, always doing what Vati expected of her with only one brazen exception; that of refusing to marry her father's choice; Niclaus Karl Niederer

Through her fixed gaze, the Monte Brè church—dazzling white—seemed to beckon. Thusly, she made an instant decision. There, she would go… alone…. Hopefully, before the American would be up.

She dressed hurriedly, ate breakfast, and told the clerk she would not be back for lunch. Then, with the verve of a conspiratorial spy, she hurried away from the hotel to a bus stop.

The sun was high as she ate lunch at a small table beneath a blue and white umbrella on the top-most terrace of Monte Brè. The view—reverse of that from the hotel—presented a breathtaking panorama. Like a great piece of blue velvet, Lago Lugano dominated the whole scene. On the right looped three beach crescents; Paradiso, directly across, then Lugano proper, and Lido, nearest to Brè. To the left, dolomitic San

Salvatore spread a short shadow like a black seal hugging its northern slope. The precipitous southern side descended abruptly into the lake, broken only by a ribbon of road cut along the base. A white steamer, trailing a soft V wake, cleaved the distant water as it aimed toward Italy. Smaller craft, like minute snowflakes, dotted the calm surface. And Beau Rivage, from such a distance, huddled inconspicuously amongst other hotels beside the road in Paradiso.

She tried to delineate it but could not. Would that she could look back and see herself... as objectively. Since she had left the hotel—except for an hour at the Evangelische Kirche—her thoughts revolved around the abject futility of her future. Her twenty-nine years loomed larger than reality. One third of her lifetime—if she were lucky, and lived as long as her ancestors. In September she would be... thirty! Thirty, thirty, thirty. It drummed repeatedly within her brain.

How easy it would be to allow Ward to love her, and... to love him in return—a summer romance, begun and ended within a week. Then, he would go his way back to the United States, and she would go her way... back to Zürich; to her home... and to Karl.

Her thoughts went back to a time before she was born. Her father and Karl's father were cousins who worked in the grocery business founded by their grandfather; Niclaus Karl Niederer the first, born on the tenth of September in 1842. When a great-grandson was born a hundred years later on the same date, and a great grand-daughter a year later, also on the same date, the fathers considered it a portentious omen which they could not ignore. So while Rosa Wyler recovered from her difficult delivery in Zürich's Frauenklinik, both men—having cause for celebration—raised high their steins of beer in solemn tribute to the stern, bewhiskered portrait of the old patriarch, and consecrated the innocent children in marriage, one to the other.

Although the Niederers lived in Basel and the Wylers in Zürich, demands of business brought them together for infrequent weekend or holiday visits.

Karl and his older sister Anna were the only children Rosina knew until she went to school. As children, they played well together until the summer when Rosina was almost fourteen.

The Niederers had come on from Basel and both families had gone for a picnic up on Zürichberg—a mountain directly behind the Wyler home. Afterward, young Karl had enticed Rosina off alone, ostensibly to visit the Zoo. But when he had her alone on a wooded path, he turned abruptly and spoke with glee. "Wow, how your tits have grown since last Easter!" And reaching out with the thumb and forefinger of each hand, through her dress, he pinched the nubile growth of both her breasts.

Indignant at the crude affront to her person, she pushed both fists hard against his chest. "You leave me alone!"

But he was stronger than she and he thrust his arms around her, pinning both arms to her sides, then forced his mouth—with crude violence—down upon hers. Escape was impossible so she kicked his leg and bit his lip.

"Damn wild cat aren't you?" he said, drawing a hand across his stinging lip. "But you just wait!. When we are married, I will play with you all I want to!" then added with a sneer, "you won't object then, my precious cousin! I'll make you feel so good… you will beg me to touch you!"

A week later—after repeated nightmares and daily loss of appetite—a frightened girl found the courage to ask her mother if that was so? Then from wife to husband, and husband to cousin, inevitably to Karl himself, came such reprimand that on their annual birthday party, a contrite boy made shamed apology to the injured girl. He gave her a pearl necklace, and she made a dutiful pretense at forgiving him. But the days of platonic carefree childhood were gone. Rosina—grown to strange new maturity—could not forget.

Through the year she met and brought home other young men. To each, Vati made it unmistakably clear that his daughter would one day marry the heir to the Niederer Grocery chain. Thus, any interested young man, quite naturally, became... disinterested.

On her nineteenth birthday she had accepted a valuable diamond ring, even though she insisted on continuing her education and subsequent career.

Karl had affairs with other girls, much to the consternation of both sets of parents who frequently upbraided the young couple for wasting their youth by such an indefinable existence.

A waitress presented the check and cleared the table. Rosina paid her. Then, like a stiff mechanical doll, she walked across the terrace onto a path—ascending an upward curve around the mountain.

She walked for a while, then stopped beside a knarled chestnut tree. From that point the lake was no longer visible. Only the distant alps commanded attention. Beyond them, she thought with a sigh of resignation, there... is my life.

Raising her eyes to the endless sky above, she asked questions for which she already knew the answers.

"Why... can I not be free? Why... can I not do what I want?"

She recalled a movie on turtles; saw the little one scramble from the confining egg and head for the water to a life of glorious freedom. Only natural inclination guided the turtle's direction. The turtle had no ancestors or parents or customs to decide for him which way to go.

Ah yes, she knew the answers; "Because I have brains and I am guided by reason... instead of instinct. Because I must have consideration for what others want and... because I am civilized. <u>Civilized</u>! Oh God!

With lagging footsteps, she went down the rise to the cable-car platform. Lengthening shadows crossed her path. In vague thought, she realized that no resolution had manifested itself upon her mind. She had enjoyed the excursion; the quiet freedom; the unrivaled beauty of varied viewpoints; and the inevitable awareness of individual insignificance... from any mountain-top.

Half a block. from the funicular base station, Rosina boarded a bus. Through the center of town it became inexorably slowed by five-o'clock traffic. After transferring to the Paradiso line—which went along the lake's perimeter—she found it no less crowded, hot or noisy than the ride through town. The inner confinement made sharp contrast beside Lake Lugano's inviting coolness.

After leaving the bus she lost no time in returning to her room, and changing into her swimsuit.

With joyous anticipation, she emerged from the hotel moving on light footsteps across the gray flagstones toward the water. Abruptly before her—as though barring the way—loomed the bright red bench. Cigar-shaped shadows—cast by tall palm-trees—lay across the quay, and one... across the back and head of Ward Fairbanks, who sat there calmly smoking his pipe. On the pavement before him he spotted her unmoving shadow. In an instant he sprang to his feet. With undue sharpness he demanded, "Where have you been all day?"

Her joyous expression had vanished. "I do not have to account to you!" she snapped.

"No, of course you don't," he apologized. "Sorry."

He was truly delighted to see her. With what he hoped was a contrite tone, he said. "I'll get changed and join you. I'll only be a minute."

It was on the tip of her tongue to quip, "It is a free lake." But the sincerity of his gaze forbade the flip words.

On a flag pole above her—framed against the Eden's silver balconies—hung a white cross upon its blood-red ground. Instinctively, she looked up as a sudden breeze whipped the flag from limp lifelessness into a broad fluttering banner. She mused over it, feeling her own vacillation between limpid acquiescence and the defiance of also hanging on against the wind. She sighed, and walked slowly along the quay and descended the stairs. She plunged into the lake, then floated idly on her back until a strange man came up beside her. At sight of a wide grin spread across a youthful face, she swam rapidly away. As she reached the yellow float, the boy caught up with her.

"Sie sind ein gut schwimmer," he said.

She climbed the ladder but did not answer him.

"Ich hoffe," he persisted, climbing up beside her, "dass Sie Deutsch verstehen? "

"Ja doch, und danke, " she answered.

Awkwardly, she continued to rebuff each parry the German boy tried. Deep within her—though she knew not why—she wished that Ward would come. When finally, she saw him enter the water, she felt a strange reassurance. Casually, she turned to the youthful admirer, and with complete nonchalance, said, "Da kommt nun mein Mann."

This information caused the intruder to jump off the platform and swim away in a quite different direction.

When Ward reached her she was still chuckling.

"Why are you so amused?" he asked as he climbed the ladder to join her.

Her eyes followed the German boy, now swimming toward the shore. "You would not understand," she answered calmly.

He followed her gaze. "Was he annoying you?"

"Oh no. He only wanted to be friendly."

She sat back, stretching out her legs and leaned back on the palms of both hands.

"I could punch him on the nose," said Ward, dropping down beside her.

"Uh, huh," she murmured, pushing off the white cap and shaking loose her hair. "You did not punch Stanley on the nose yesterday… on the train."

He looked at the slightly raised eyebrows above a twinkling amusement in her dark blue eyes. "Didn't have to. You cut him down to size yourself."

"Precisely." She answered. With that, she lay back on the hard surface, one arm folded beneath her head, the other, palm upward, across her eyes.

Ward, half supported by one elbow, studied the form beside him. Only her nose, lips and chin showed below her arm. While above it, hair, spread out like brown silk, spilled over her other wrist. His gaze swept down across the curve of breast to another curve of hip line. Although he knew she could not observe his rapt appraisal, he dared look no longer. For there comes a point at which a man... any man, becomes unable... to control his hands!

He lay back on the yellow canvas—shielding his own eyes against the sun.

"You... a... did not give me the cold-shoulder treatment?"

"No."

"Why not?"

"I don't know."

"Will you tell me why... you kept me waiting all day?"

She thought for a moment—trying to formulate an honest answer. "I wanted to spend the day alone. You see, today was the first time... I have ever gone anywhere... by myself. I know that sounds strange... coming from one who is my age, but it is so. My parents hardly let me out of their sight, except to go to work. When I decided to make this trip, they were so troubled and hurt, I very nearly canceled it. But..." she went on with deep emotion, "I had to do it! I really did!"

"No dates?" he asked. "No men in your life?"

"Only one...." She hesitated, wondering how to explain Karl in the fewest possible words. "A distant cousin..." She took in a deep breath, "... whom my parents expect me to marry."

He turned to look at her. "But you don't want to?"

"I would rather not discuss it!"

She had, he reflected, answered the question to his complete satisfaction. Secretly delighted by the insight into her transient behavior, and the fact that she was not in love with anyone else, he envisioned no insurmountable problem. It was quite simple. From now on he would be firm.

He reached over, running his fingers through her hair and along the side of her head. This caused her to turn her face and look at him from beneath her sheltering hand.

He subdued the urge to kiss her by suggesting that they swim back and get dressed for dinner. Having—by himself—concluded some important decisions, he suddenly felt ravenously hungry.

Rosina put on the other new dress; a light peach color, which she had bought the same time as the green one especially for this vacation. Then, glancing at her watch, she knew she had time to telephone home. "Yes, she was having a good time. No, she would not get sunburned. Yes, she had been to church. No, she would not talk to strange men, (Quick prayer of forgiveness there) And No! she would absolutely not come home until next Sunday."

So—ten minutes later—with a secretive, most delightful air of one who is about to eat the forbidden fruit, she walked out of the lift to where Ward stood waiting for her.

He *is* striking, she thought with quick perception, appraising his beige sport jacket and a brown necktie, which set off an attractive, though not handsome face. The effect upon her caused a most unusual flipping inside her breast.

In the same manner he absorbed all of her; the peach colored dress; the right amount of make-up and shining hair, rolled and brushed to its best advantage. His eyes held hers for a long moment.

"You make a lovely picture, Rosina."

Unaccustomed to praise, she sought to hide the thrill of his words by a light rejoinder. "It is rather marvelous what a new dress and a little make-up can accomplish."

"Oh definitely," he agreed, walking beside her across the dining-room, "when there is beautiful raw material to work with."

Embarrassment flushed through her. Karl never used words like lovely, or beautiful. A startling awareness sharpened her senses as she discerned Ward's deft movements; guiding her with the ease of a splendid animal out on the terrace to a particular table, gripping long fingers around the back of her chair; lowering his tall body gracefully into the one opposite; then, with a casual smile, accepting the menus offered by a white-jacketed waiter.

"I assume," he asked her, "that Italian is one of your languages? I feel stupid asking the waiter to translate everything but the word spaghetti."

"I do not speak Italian, but the food is not difficult to understand."

"No? What is Polenta? What is Mortadella?"

"Polenta is a type of dumpling. Mortadella is sausage." she answered.

"What I would like, if you can find it, is roast lamb." he said.

"That is the Agnello arrosto. Risotto goes well with it, if you like rice and onions."

"Yes, thank you." He did not look up. "I suppose I'll be safe with minestrone? Last night when I got to the bottom of my soup dish, it was full of snails."

She exploded with laughter, giving him a look of sympathetic amusement. "You do not like snails?"

He responded with a wry smile, then he too had to laugh.

When the waiter returned Rosina ordered for both Ward and herself. She also asked about the local wine.

"Nostrano or Asti?"

"The Nostrano, please."

He returned immediately with fragrant vegetable soup, explained that risotto took about twenty minutes, then disappeared.

"Now," said Ward, between spoonfuls, "tell me where you went today."

She tasted the soup, then turned to look at Monte Brè, where scattered houses sparkled in tiny squares lit by a setting sun. "Up there on that pretty little mountain, the view is superb."

"No doubt. It is magnificent from the one behind this hotel, San Salvatore. That is where I went," he added with a slight edge in his voice, "alone!"

"Where was Stanley?"

"With the Verlindes. Bergit told Stan they were going on the lake steamer and he happened to take the same boat."

Ward ate his soup and watched Roslna. Her eyes looked downward as she ate. He saw only their dark-fringed lashes blinking intermittently.

She felt his gaze upon her and dared not look up. His empty dish was safer refuge. "No snails in the soup?" she asked lightly.

"Didn't find any."

She smiled. Only then did she meet his gaze.

"You are beautiful when you smile. Not that you are not beautiful when you don't, but I like the smile better."

His words caused a thump in her chest which spread heat through her throat up into her cheeks.

"You are full of compliments this evening, Sir. I should reciprocate by telling you how much I like that jacket and tie."

At that moment the waiter brought salad and wine, whisked away the soup plates and poured some wine for Ward to taste. He then produced a heaping platter of roast lamb in neat, layered slices over a bed of steaming risotto. Using two spoons in one hand, he piled a little of each onto their plates, bowed with a slight nod for the Signorina, the Signore, and moved discreetly away.

Ward poured the wine, then raised his glass to Rosina.

"Thank you for being here. Believe me, it makes all the difference in the world having someone like you across from me… at dinner." Before he had finished speaking, the delectable odor of onions assailed his nostrils. He took a deep breath, savoring the delightful piquancy, and began to eat with relish. He drank the dry red wine and found it satisfying. The idea occurred to him that it was well she ate onions too, for tonight there would be no nonsense like a brief kiss on her forehead.

On the verge of a new life, he reflected upon a strange truth: He had never really wanted to marry any of the women he had known. Even though, on more than one occasion… he had come damn close!

When they had finished, the waiter cleared the table, then placed before them: whole strawberries, thin wedges of soft white cheese and black demitasse.

Rosina took only the coffee, but Ward helped himself with gusto.

"You can eat so much, yet stay so slim?" she asked.

"I've had a busy day, walking all over that mountain, then swimming, and…" he paused as a gentle, flower-scented breeze wafted across the terrace. "… this glorious air… I know I shall go home with an extra ten pounds."

"You can stand it."

"Of course. I will merely let my belt out a notch."

He ate the last strawberry, then asked, "What would you like to do now?"

"Now?"

She looked out across the lake in a sweeping glance northward, toward the town center. The magic hour of twilight hung suspended in air, spiked here and there by flicks of oncoming lights. Then, like a great gray curtain, darkness dropped lightly over the blue-green jade of lake and mountains.

"I would like to walk along the quay…," she decided, standing up to see it all more clearly. An ethereal vision, as more lights stung the dusk, lifted her out of the mundane into fairyland as day moved casually into night. "I would like to follow the lights, on and on and on…" Overcome by sublime emotion, she added softly, "… until there are no more."

Ward, standing beside her—looking down at the nut-brown silken head—felt his eyelids sting, his heart constrict, and tightened lungs hold their air.

For more than an hour they walked, stopping frequently to gaze at lake and mountains, lights and sky, in all their rare and varied beauty. He held her hand, squeezing it from time to time.

At a central plaza where a multi-streamed fountain sprayed fronds of bright water into the night air, Rosina stopped. "How beautiful!" she exclaimed, looking down at the circle of an irridescently green pool into which it fell. The gentle swish of water blended with blatant traffic cacophony and softer voices of the night. A thousand feet distant, misty celestial glimmers emanated from hotel marquee lights.

Ward's arm lay across Rosina's shoulder. Caught up in the magic of suspended time, they stood so for several minutes. "Yes," he agreed. "It is beautiful!"

Then taking her arm, he led her through the heavy traffic across the street and up into the old town. They walked through narrow crooked streets, pausing now and then to admire displays in the lighted windows of closed shops. Once they drifted into a dim cafe for a cool drink.

Lured by untrod ways, they explored even further. Ward read all the street names with obvious delight; Via, Vegezzi, Luvini, Frasca, Pestalozzi, Bossi and Pretorlo. To herself Rosina marveled at how a man could find joy in such a simple natural pastime. Hours passed; wonder-filled, enchanting hours.

They gradually circled back toward the quay where Ward spied a most appealing sign: TAXI. "Yonder, my fleet-footed friend, I see an end to our pedestrian wanderings, for I will run out of foot-power long before you run out of lights."

"Please, let's take one more look at the colored fountains in the lake!" she begged. "Then we can take a taxi."

If, in the same breath, she had asked for a ride to the moon, he would have tried to arrange passage.

Close beside the lake where it was dark, Rosina stood still. From behind her, Ward's strong arms encircled her waist and pulled her back against his chest. His chin rested lightly against her hair as they gazed with rapt fascination at five luminous geysers—more than seventy feet high—which splayed water into the lake.

"They are such gorgeous colors," she whispered. "I wonder how it is done."

"I think there is a colored spot-light beside each jet-stream."

"Like an open fire, it has a mesmerizing effect."

"In which each beholder sees something different. For instance, what do you see?"

"Meters and meters of colored chiffon. And you?"

"Well… the yellow is the dress you wore on the train. The green is the one you wore last night. The light peach is what you have on now. The blue is the color of your eyes,

"And the violet?"

"That one…," he said, turning her around to face him, "… has to be changed to brown! The color of your hair."

He placed a hand beneath her chin, lifted her face up to his, and bent to kiss her lips. His fingers coursed upward through thick, silky hair to support her head against the pressure of his own. At first—tender and gently—he savored the delicate rapturous feeling that spread throughout his body. But when her hands moved voluntarily across his back, he pressed harder, more ardently, ever closer into incalculable, careless abandon. He held her thus, longer than he intended, for simultaneously, to both of them came deep, exalted uncontrollable breathing.

Instinctively sensing a danger of such rapt abandon in so public a place, he straightened and drew her head protectively against his shoulder. "Oh Rosina, you are so… so wonderful," he whispered against her ear.

"B… but," she interrupted, "I am afraid that…."

"Afraid! … of what? … of me?"

"No. Afraid that you will like me too much," she answered in a voice hardly above a whisper.

"Like you!" he burst out. "Like you! You dear, sweet, adorable… angel!" But, as he bent to kiss her again, she pulled away, knowing quite well that a fuse had been lighted which had to either burn—as it surely could into ultimate explosion, or… be quickly extinguished!

"We had better go find that taxi," she said with decision.

Silently, they retraced the distance back to the taxi stand. Each savored a new feeling of awareness for the other. His, of having found someone who made the word love a reality. Hers, of unfathomable inner turmoil.

Somewhere, a clock struck twelve times—with deep resounding reverberation—Just as it had done for many nights throughout the past century.

Six B

Jeanette Bondt hated Sundays. They stretched before her in endless, nonproductive, nondemanding hours. Since the ski vacation with Wilhelm, she abhorred them even more. It had been his habit to call her Sunday evenings, either to make plans, or just to talk; to relate day by day activities, or to remind her how much he loved her; how much he missed her.

The first three months she had waited... every Sunday... for a phone that did not ring. When Easter came, she had gone home to Wallisellen, and taken her mother and aunt to church, remaining there until late at night. She learned that staying away from her apartment, wondering, was little better than being there... listening. However, purposeful activity proved to be far better than aimless waiting. Thus a Sunday excursion or visit became mandatory. She had few friends, and only four relatives; her mother and aunt in Wallisellen, and her mother's cousin; Rosa, and Rosa's daughter, Rosina, here in Zürich. But Rosa's husband, Johann, who disapproved Jeanette's unconventional existence these many years, laid no welcome mat for her upon his doorstep.

On this particular Sunday, the sixth of June, she looked through her window down to a patch of Zürichsee glistening serene and pale blue in the morning sun. "I believe I will take the steamer to Rapperswil," she said aloud. "I have not done that for several years."

On that same morning, Otto Lander, from his terrace on the hillside east of Zürichsee, stood looking down across the same sparkling blue water to the verdant hills beyond. Southward, to his left, snow-capped Alps rose in peaks of whipped egg-whites. The previous day's storm left the air clean and cool, permitting an unusually clear vista. He took a deep breath and reached out subconsciously to put an arm around a wife, who was no longer there, who would never be there again. Tears of loneliness stung his eyes.

Then, because he also gazed westerly toward Bern, where his eldest daughter lived, he made an instant decision. "I will go to visit Elizabeth," he said aloud. "It is more than two months now since I have seen those grandchildren."

It was almost eleven when Otto returned home that night. He drank his nightly shot of brandy and dropped into bed exhausted. After an hour of tossing and turning, he went down the stairs of his big house for another brandy. Grumpy, from a day that had not been all he anticipated, he felt old. Certainly too old to keep up with four spirited grandchildren. Too old to be comfortable with a beautiful daughter, so very like her mother. And, too damned old to drive that distance in one day. But, he thought, as he climbed back into bed, feeling new warmth from the brandy, not too old to wish for a woman in his house, <u>and</u> in his bed! With sudden impulse, he reached for his glasses, then for the phone book, and then the telephone.

Jeanette had taken the last boat back from Rapperswil. Going across the quay, she had met some friends who suggested she join them for a drink. Shortly before midnight, she made her excuses, and called a taxi.

The telephone began to ring as she turned the key in the door of her apartment. "Oh God" she breathed, flicking on a light and crossing the room to where it tolled insistently for the third time. With trembling hands, she picked it up.

"Jeanette Bondt here," she answered with bated breath.

"Did I wake you? I know it is very late, Jeanette, … but I could not sleep." Otto said in a rush of words.

And she, breathing normally once more, answered, "No, Otto, I just came in."

Disconcerted by the probability that she had been out with a man, he became, for the moment, dissuaded from his mission. "Were you… " he hesitated, "… out with a friend?"

"No, Otto, alone."

"All evening… all day?"

She breathed a sigh of resignation. "Yes, all evening and all day… except for a late drink with friends of mine."

"I too, was alone all day, except for this afternoon which I spent with Elizabeth's family in Bern. It is a long drive, alone. "

"You must be tired, " she soothed, beginning to wonder why he had phoned.

"Yes, tired of driving. "

"You are over-tired, that is why you cannot get to sleep."

He could have pointed out that she was 100 percent wrong there, but that would have been too blatant.

"Perhaps," he said doubtfully, thinking; What a damned waste, her being all alone in that apartment!

So, in the aggressive manner he used in his position of managing director, he asked, "What evening this week can you go out to dinner with me?"

"Why Otto, how nice," she said with surprised delight. Any evening you wish."

"Tomorrow?"

"All right."

"I will stop by your office. Auf Wiedersehen."

"Auf Wiedersehen."

The old grandfather clock in the downstairs hall of Otto's house struck twelve o'clock, but Otto was fast asleep before the final count.

Six C

In Freiburg, Germany, that same evening, Doctor Wilhelm Gottfried and his wife attended a party given by the parents of their daughter Marlene's fiance. During the ride home, Henrietta—who had imbibed too freely from the punch bowl—brazenly broke the awkward silence with a strange request.

"After Marlene's wedding, I want a divorce. There will no longer be any reason to keep on with our sham marriage!"

"Eh?" he glanced at her in astonishment, wondering what she really had in mind. He turned the car from the highway onto the boulevard.

"Then you can marry your Swiss girlfriend and I can travel." she added with smug satisfaction, "around the world, I think."

"All alone, I suppose?"

"Of course not. I will go with a tour."

"You have money for all that?" he asked with biting sarcasm.

"What I don't have, you will pay for!"

"Oh, you think so!" he spat out angrily. His fingers gripped the wheel tighter than necessary.

"Yes," she retorted, "I think so! The price for your Swiss mistress is going to be high!"

Wilhelm felt a tingling in his arms and legs. No price, he realized, would be too high to be rid of her!

He thought back over the thirty year period since he had married. Long years, frustrating for them both, were climaxed by her angry reproach the day after his return from Arosa in January. "How was the skiing?" she had asked. Suspecting nothing amiss, he had answered, "Excellent."

"And your Swiss companion, does she ski well? Or is she just good in bed?" Instinctively, he remembered her gossipy friend.

"When you plunge the knife, you push deep," he answered angrily.

With a biting sneer she countered, "I can also turn it!" Releasing long pent-up venom, she went on. "I know all about your affair… have known about it for years."

"I am sorry," he had said, utterly defeated.

"Sorry!" she cried. Her voice rose to hissing tone of acrimony. "You stay away from that bitch, or you will be truly… sorry!"

He ignored the insult, only because he knew there was no point in pursuing it. He also knew that she meant it. She could ruin his practice and his standing in the community. But worst of all, she would try to alienate his daughter, Marlene, the lovely child who should have been his and… Jeanette's.

What should he do about Jeanette? The only thing he could, under the circumstances; get along without her, keeping busy, busy, busy! And ultimately, through daily resolve, forget about her… for all time!

On more than one Sunday evening, he had gone to his office, intending to telephone. Instead he sat in abject silence, eventually convincing himself it was better not to. It never once occurred to him, that by such a decision, without explanation, he stretched Jeanette across a rack of torture more cruel than the four-horse tearing asunder in medieval times.

On this Sunday night in June, while Henrietta waited for Willy to unlock the door, she asked, "What time is it? My watch has stopped."

He pushed back the cuff of his left wrist and answered, "Twelve o'clock."

6 D

In Basel, a young man who had been drinking more than he should, drove with careful determination along deserted streets toward his home in Riehen-bei-Basel, close to the border of France. That morning—after shaving his ruggedly handsome face, combing his black, curly hair, admiring his own husky physique, and feeling quite satisfied with himself—he had phoned Rosina to tell her he was driving down to Zürich. The news that she was gone—for a whole week—along with a refusal to tell him where, had so infuriated Karl Niederer he almost forgot to say a polite, "Thank you. I will come down next Sunday." He <u>had</u> remained in control—for only that long!

Clenching both his teeth and his fists, he hissed, angrily, "She cannot do this to me!"

Still seething, he reviewed his list of girl friends and telephoned the most acquiescent—the one who would refuse him nothing.

However, the long day, spent with an empty-headed Fraulein, whose only attributes were fun and sex, had in no way helped his deflated ego.

In his driveway, he turned off the car's ignition and stared absently through the windshield. Excusing his boorish behavior, he rationalized, "I would have no need of… trollops… if Rosina were not such an icicle!"

He recalled how two weeks earlier they had discussed quite frankly their feelings for each other. She had asked why he did not find someone who could be a more loving, responsive wife.

"Because it is you I want! It is you I love!"

"But Karl," she responded with utter desolation, "I do not feel like that. I have no passionate response to your embrace."

"You would, if you would let me show you," he coaxed. "You could be different. You could… love me."

He remembered how she had stiffened as he swept his hand between her thighs and whispered in her ear, "Please… let me try?"

Her repeated, almost hysterical, "No, no, no!" still rang in his ears.

Now he bent over to look at the dashboard clock.

Thinking aloud, he vowed with vehemence! "Damn her passive resistance! Next time I get her alone, I won't take any… no, no, no! I will show her who is boss!"

Then, blinking his eyes to see more clearly, he finally observed that both hands on the luminous dial pointed straight upward.

6 E

Rosina had telephoned while Johann and Rosa were eating a light supper of homemade bread, Muenster cheese, and red wine. In unbearable silence, they finished—each conveying to the other a feeling of utter emptiness.

Rosa then busied herself cleaning up, while Johann sat smoking a pipe, rocking his chair back and forth with an incessant squeak. Hours ticked by in slow measured clicks until it grew dark. Then with a tiredness which comes from the utter disparity of doing nothing, they moved—by force of habit—into their bedroom.

Both lay wide awake thinking horrible, accusatory, self-defeating thoughts.

It bothered Johann that he could not tell Karl where Rosina had gone. It was not right. She was a willful, ungrateful, stubborn girl! It was certainly not what she should be doing! But what could he do? He could not lock her up and she was too old for a strapping!

And Rosa, who desperately wished for lots of grandchildren before she died, saw them only in fantasy; adorable little girls and a cuddly newborn boy, seeing again and again her own dead babies which had aborted before their time. Rosina's birth had come safely through full term only because a specialist insisted that Rosa spend her last three months in bed—a decree which is tantamount to prison for a Swiss Hausfrau, when kept from her innate cleaning, cooking and gardening.

Lying awake in the darkness, they shared their ignoble thoughts, which only heightened their fear and frustration. They were certain that their daughter, off doing "God know what!" all by herself, would be accosted by strange men, most certainly by raped! and would come to no good end!

Finally, Rosa slipped from bed and went to the kitchen to prepare warm milk which would help them both to sleep.

Returning with two cups, she handed one to Johann as tears rolled down her cheeks. "She was such a beautiful baby… always such a great joy…."

"So good, too!" responded Johann, nodding his head. "Such a good girl… always doing what she was told" He went on, disillusion tinging his voice. "Until these last few years when she has become… so difficult! All I want is what is best for her, and she…" he paused in confusion, shaking his head back and forth, "she does not want it at all."

"The pity of it is," said Rosa, "she does not know *what* she wants!"

"Exactly! Which is why we must insist upon the wedding… right after she gets home!"

"She does not want a wedding," offered the timid Rosa.

Johann finished his milk, handed her the cup, saying, "Karl will get tired of waiting, then you know what will happen to her?" He lay down, drawing the quilt up around his neck while Rosa waited in fearful apprehension, for him to go on. "She will get to be just like your cousin's daughter, that Jeanette."

"Oh no!" she breathed, then added vehemently, "No, Johann, you are wrong!"

Surprised, he sat up again; his voice became harsh with disbelief. "Eh, What's this? me, wrong?"

She sat down beside him to soothe his bristled attitude, to try to make him understand something.

"Last month when I told her we would make a wedding this month, she acted like a frightened animal. When I told her it was past time—at twenty nine—to begin to making babies… you know what she told me?

That she could not bear the thought of it. And I said, 'Which, the birthing… or the making?' And you may not want to believe this, but she said, 'The making is what I cannot bear the thought of,' and then she smiled and said, 'Mutti, birthing them would be… marvelous!' Now I ask you, Johann, is that any way for a normal healthy girl to be?"

Then in the semi-darkness she watched Johann's face grow pale, his jaw drop, and his eyes bulge in their sockets.

She took the cups back to the kitchen, reiterating her conviction with numb pathos. "Rosina is too cold to allow a man to touch her. No, she will not be like Jeanette, absolutely not! Jeanette has not had babies, but she… knows what it is… to love a man."

From long subconscious habit, Rosa rinsed out the cups and glanced at the clock on the wall. It was midnight.

Chapter Seven

The following morning, Rosina sang, "Oh, what a beau-ti-ful Morn-ing!" as she rifled through her clothes for a violet colored outfit. Oh, what a beau-ti-ful day." as she pulled the pants up over her hips. "I've got a won-der-ful feel-ing." while she slipped her arms into the jersey top. "Every-thing's..." She caught her reflection in the mirror and finished with slow, tune-less words, "go-ing my way." She shrugged her shoulders and talked to her reflection. "Maybe not everything for ever and ever, but surely for the next six days!"

The mood of gay exhilaration, warm and vibrant, still coursed through her as she stood beside the lift and pushed the down button. The elevator door opened.

To her surprise, Ward and Stanley stood inside, Ward, his eyes sparkling a gay message, greeted her with a flourishing, "Good morning, Miss Switzerland."

"Good morning," she answered, stepping in between them, then continued in wide-eyed innocence, "How are you both enjoying Lugano?"

"Great. Absolutely great," answered Stanley, who had had the hotel room to himself last evening, and Bergit had been a most accommodating guest.

Ward's answer reflected in his eyes—an admiring absorption of a delightful creature costumed in mauve and white. He whispered in her ear, "I could not have changed that jet fountain to brown."

"I knew that last night."

"Do you also know that I had a wonderful time last night?"

"Yes. So did I."

Bergit joined them for breakfast and afterward the four vacationers walked along Via Dei le Scuole to the San Salvatore funicular. For Ward had generously invited them all atop 'his mountain'.

From one of the rectangular windows cut like stairs in the side of a bright red train, Ward looked over Rosina's head at Monte Brè. "Tomorrow morning we will go up 'your mountain'."

"Not in the morning," she said. "I am going to a concert in the park at eleven. If we are to go up Brè together it will have to be in the afternoon."

"Concert in the morning. Monte Brè in the afternoon." he decided. "That," he added confidently, "takes care of Tuesday."

How easily he makes plans for me, she thought, and how passively I accept. She pondered this seemingly irresistible force… as though she wanted it that way. She recalled the passionate embraces of last night which ended with a final kiss outside her door. And how she had slept—curled up like a kitten—hugging her knees in inexplicable joy.

Leaving the train, everyone dispersed along well trod paths. Stan and Bergit chose to walk upward to a chapel on the summit—where old stone arches would provide secluded nooks. But Ward and Rosina traversed a lower ridge which provided its own seclusion.

The view—from where they stood embraced all the arms of Lake Lugano, surrounded by green, wooded slopes, which in a northerly direction became purple mountains merging into snow-capped alps. Ward laid a hand upon Rosina's shoulder. Involuntarily, she folded her arm up to place her fingers over his. Silent, transcendental waves of understanding passed between then. Time—because they willed it so—stood still. But the clocks of the world ticked on.

He directed her attention to the concentration of distant buildings which comprised the center of Lugano. "It tends to make you feel insignificant, doesn't it?" he asked.

She nodded assent, for even a spoken yes could not get past the lump in her throat.

After what seemed like such a short space of time, Stan called down to the statue-like forms so engrossed in the view, and in the world, and in each other.

"Hey, you two. It's past twelve, and we're hungry."

"O. K." Ward answered agreeably, while actually despising the call back to reality. "We'll meet you at the train."

He smiled down at Rosina and bent to kiss that which was nearest, the end of her nose.

"Shall we go back to earth, angel?"

"Yes sir. As soon as I fold up my wings."

During lunch, Ward asked if she would help him with some shopping.

"Shopping?"

"Surely you remember all those closed shops last night."

"Oh, yes, of course."

When he suggested a taxi, she said, "It costs less to ride the bus."

"And even less to walk." He gave her a side-long glance. "But if you think for one minute that I'm going to walk to town after walking ten miles last night...."

"We did not walk ten miles!" she scoffed. "It was certainly not more than four!"

"How about a compromise?" he asked. "Go on the bus, come back in a taxi?"

She answered with a gay chuckle. Her eyes flashing acceptance.

They entered a shop which featured delicate embroidered blouses. "What size," he asked Rosina, "should I get for two girls, one eight, the other ten?"

So he is married, she thought. How strange I did not sense it before. "How big are the girls?" she asked.

Ward looked puzzled for a moment. "Big?" he asked. And because he had not seen his nieces since Christmas, he tried to remember. "I don't know. I thought you could help me. Don't you know how big girls are at that age?"

"I will try. We can estimate large, and they will grow into them." She discussed it with the sales girl. A decision was made.

He took the sales slip and paid the cashier. Then, returning to where Rosina waited, he exchanged the receipt for the package, and they left the store.

Finding it impossible to dodge around people sauntering along the crowded sidewalk, they took to the cobble-stoned street.

Deep within her, Rosina fought against an overwhelming depression. Finally she formed the words which had to be said, "Your little girls should like your choice. Those are lovely blouses."

"My little girls!" he responded with incredulous, surprise, "I don't have...." Abruptly, he turned to face her, preventing her from moving. "Did you think... these were for children of mine?" His eyes, like steel balls, bored into her with unrelenting ferocity.

"H... how would I know she answered, feeling helpless and truly grievous. "It seemed natural to assume the blouses were for...."

He cut her short. "Let's find a place where we can talk instead of this busy street."

They continued down the steep cobbled way in silence walking until they found a bench near the lake.

"Now look at me, Rosina and answer me truthfully."

"Yes?"

"Do you think I would have kissed you as I did last night, or even be here with you now, it I were married?"

"I... I..." she stammered, trying to apologize. A tight constriction pressed hard fingers inside her throat. She stared at Ward's knees, at brown tweed flecked with green. She had been the one guilty of duplicity… for she was engaged to be married!

Studying her downcast eyes, her trembling lip, he knew he had caused her pain and should not pursue the question. He cursed the bright afternoon sunlight; the too public piazza filled with strolling people. He would have gathered her close and spilled out all his love had they been in the privacy of blessed darkness. With loving tenderness, he laid his arm across her tensed shoulders.

"Something more grave than this… mistaken conclusion is bothering you, Rosina. What is it?"

At first, she looked away, far down the lake. But when he took her hand, she relaxed and began to talk. Pent up words tumbled out in rapid expression of her troubled thoughts. She told him about her parents, her life at home, her relationship with Karl. During her monologue, he became fascinated by the purple color of her slacks. It gave cognizance to the incredible coincidence of decadent royalty. Several questions nagged him, but he did not interrupt.

Then she paused—lifting her eyes to him—he asked the first one. "If your great-grandfather was also Karl's great-grandfather, why then are you not as much heir to the family business and money as he is?"

"Because Karl's grandfather, being a man, took over the development of the business. My grandmother, Anna Niederer, married my grandfather, Caspar Wyler, who owned a farm in the Glatt Valley east of Zürich."

"So your father became a farmer like his father?"

"No. He left the farm to go to Zürich and work for his uncle. Karl's father, Albert, and Albert's twin brother Niclaus, both went to the University. Because they had a higher education, they branched out and eventually spread super-markets all over Switzerland. At the same time, they revised the long name, Kolonialwarenhandler to Kolonialmarkt. Karl's father managed the import office in Basel; his brother Niclaus the headquarters in Zürich. Uncle Niclaus is unmarried, so Karl is the only male heir, Karl has an older sister Anna, but she has four daughters."

Rosina turned away to look at distant mountains as she went on to explain about her father. "He had no higher education. He never learned any language but German, so he did not progress out of the shipping department."

"Now, he is retired?" Ward asked.

"Oh no. He is seventy-five, but he will not retire as long as he has good health."

Ward thought of his own father, who at sixty-nine had been retired for four years.

He now asked the most pertinent question, for he had to know the answer. "Why do you let everyone force you into a marriage you don't want?"

"They are not <u>forcing</u> me!"

"No? What would you call it?"

"I must do what my father thinks is best for me. And I will do it... some day."

"Rubbish."

"What does that mean?"

"Nonsense!" He clarified it further. "What you are saying makes no damned sense at all."

"Please, you do not understand." she entreated.

"You're so right! I don't!" His voice stung with reprimand. He went on irritably, "You have brains enough to hold a good job... and you are certainly old enough to make your own decisions. You just haven't got the spunk to stand up and tell them all off!"

"Perhaps an American girl can do that..." She stood up, looked down the lake toward Paradiso, and finished with resignation, "... but I am Swiss!" (By which she meant to convey a whole philosophy which he would never comprehend.)

Ward restrained himself from saying, nuts, to avoid making the same translation as rubbish.

In the taxi he stared at the innocent package on his lap. "These..." he stated, in order to clear up the situation, "... are for my nieces, Debbie and Terry."

"I understand. " She spoke softly, in meek subordination. "I am sorry I was so... stupid."

Ward said nothing. His deep consternation evolved—not from any... stupid conclusion, but from her unmitigated stubbornness.

Late that night, when he kissed her good-night, and she responded with warmth and tenderness, he became more confused than ever. But, he had to admit, he was no longer angry.

Although he had been in bed for more than an hour, at two in the morning, Ward still had not slept. Quietly, so as not to disturb the sleeping Stanley—he went out on the balcony, lowered himself into a chair, and lit up his pipe. He spent the next hour puffing away, while serious thought engaged his reason.

That evening they had gone back in town to see "Fiddler on the Roof." Afterward—seated on their usual red bench—they discussed the strange parallel between Tievy—the Russian father—and the subsequent independence of his several daughters. Because of the argument, Ward believed he <u>had</u> convinced her on some specific points. Given the right circumstances, would she also defy her father?

Logic—in the manner of wishful thinking—cast a few wisps into the rings of smoke. "She has everything I want in a wife, except... self-determination. However, she <u>did</u> assert enough independence to make a career for herself, and she <u>did</u> make this trip... against her father's wishes. Who knows? ... perhaps...."

He puffed away, drawing rapidly through the stem of his pipe, contemplating a much better day on the morrow.

Chapter Eight

In the Parco Civico, on Tuesday morning, Ward and Rosina found chairs on the outer fringe of the audience in seats which offered them the greatest privacy. Ward tilted his head at an angle which allowed him to admire Rosina, and at the same time, casually watch the orchestra. Her face in profile presented a relaxed study of dream like absorption. She might have been alone, so concentrated was her attention. The music—though soft and mellow—was strangely vibrant.

She likes this better than cabaret music, and—he thought with delight—so do I.

The first presentation, Oberon Overture, by Weber, came to a conclusion. After applause died out, the musicians launched into a plaintive melody; Debussy's L'Angolo dei Bambini. A smell of jasmine, honeysuckle, and roses, hung in the perfumed air.

He reached for Rosina's hand and pressed it. She returned the pressure with her own. His pressure spread warm tentacles of joy along her arm and into her heart. From behind closed eyes her thoughts drifted from the time on the train, when she first became aware that this was a man distinct from other men, that each experience—whether dancing, swimming, or just walking beside him—caused her thoughts to exclude everyone else… well, almost every one!

She pondered over her overwhelming eagerness for each new day and the quite obvious fact that he was just as eager to be with her. She longed constantly, for the warmth of his embrace and the stir of passion when he kissed her. The uninvited, frightening revelation that she had never felt such emotion for Karl pierced a cold icicle into the transient reverie. Oh! It was too complex to analyze. She would mull it over no longer.

I will accept it for what it is. And when it is over, I will remember it always as a pleasant piece-de resistance of a wonderful holiday. She turned her face to his with a warm, musing expression in her eyes.

The sight of his unsmiling eyes searching her own, suddenly caused her whole body to quiver. How to fathom what she read there. Admiration? Surely. Attraction? No doubt of that! Desire? Yes; for that is… part of it all. Over the latter thought, she felt a flush of blood in her face as she wondered what she would do about it… when it actually came to that.

Ward had to look away to keep from bending over and kissing the lovely eyelids. Even so, her gaze, like an indelible imprint, remained implanted in his vision.

The conductor's down-spread hands closed final notes of the suite. Applause—though necessary to the orchestra—seemed superfluous to Ward. Besides, he had no intention of releasing her hand.

Raised arms again hushed a restless audience into rapt attention, then expressively guided the violins in dainty tones before sweeping into the rhythmical, flying tempo of Strauss' Rosenkavalier Waltz.

Ward felt it's rhythm vibrate through their clenched hands. Insistent questions coursed through his mind. Does she love me? Would she marry me? Would she leave this grandiose country… for mine?

An involuntary wave of shame about some aspects of the United States flashed indigenous comparisons through his conscience. But the joyous music cast aside the abject reflections in favor of truly inherent pride in his native land.

When the lively music closed in a frenzied crescendo of drums, trumpets, full orchestra, and vibrant roll of tympany, Ward released her hand to join the audience in final exuberant applause. He watched—with joyous delight—the animated elation on Rosina's face.

"I'm so glad we came," he said as they both stood up.

"Oh yes," she responded. "I want to come every day."

"Your slightest wish, lovely princess, is my command." Then with a slight bow of his head, he took her hand and with a sweep of the other, continued, "Now, we will enter the gilded coach and ride majestically to the top of Monte Brè."

"Better if we walk a few blocks and take the funicular."

To prove the point, she directed him along a gravel path between beds of flowers.

Ward laughed. "That music didn't stay with you for very long. Walk Indeed! I intend to fly!"

Carried along by his spontaneous energy, she enjoined, "The way to fly is straight ahead, turn right at the church, cross the canal, and follow the wide avenue; Castagnola. I… will try to keep up with you."

"Hah. You have no choice. I won't let go of your hand."

Passing the church, he sobered a little. "Is this the one you… came to on Sunday?"

"Yes."

"Is it Protestant… or Catholic?"

Instinct touched a nerve in her brain. Why did he want to know that? She answered calmly, "Protestant."

"I wish I had known… I would have gone with you."

"You should not spend all of your time in Lugano… with me."

"That depends on you, whether or not… you want me to."

They had approached an area of tennis courts. Her eyes focused on a white ball soaring through the air. "I enjoy being with you." She did not take her eyes off the ball as it whammed back across the court. "You have a way of making me feel… well, special."

"I believe you are… special. You are beautiful, exciting, absolutely delightful, and…" his voice dropped to a rapt, solemn tone, "it is a distinct pleasure… to be near you."

They had approached a spot where the lake was again visible.

"Across there," Rosina pointed to the opposite shore, "is Paradiso."

"I said…."

"Yes, I heard you. But you embarrass me. I was not… looking for compliments."

"You did not get… compliments. You got… the truth."

She began walking faster. "We turn at the next corner. The funicular is not far from there."

In silence they walked up via Pico to the entrance. After a short wait, they moved—along with several other persons—into a car whose floor was a series of broad steps.

Rosina moved up front to stand and watch the steep ascent. Close behind, Ward placed a hand upon her shoulder. His chin grazed the top of her hair. As their car went up, another car came down. Two fellows in the down-car waved to her. She raised an arm and waved back.

"Rosina," he spoke softly beside her ear. "Hasn't it occurred to you that you make me… feel special too?"

Her hand reached up to touch his long fingers. She sighed. "We get off here and change cars."

"You have," he said with slight annoyance, "the darndest habit of changing the subject."

"I have many other… bad habits, too."

Amid the bustle of changing cars, Ward had no chance to pursue the matter.

On the mountain-side—between towers of green cedar—yellow jasmine, red roses, and broad-leaved laurel splashed a palette of color against a dominant back-drop of cerulean blue. Ward became deeply engrossed in taking pictures.

At the final platform, when they stepped from the car, Ward drew in a deep breath of sharp, cool air. "Lead the way to food, Angel. I'm starved!"

He followed her up to the open-air restaurant—perched like a large platter close to the mountain's top—to where the view spread out below like all-encompassing, "Cinerama."

One table beside the railing was free so they threaded their way past blue-checkered table-tops to claim it for their own.

From a few hundred feet above, thousands of amateur and professional photographers have captured the classic view. Later, Ward asked Rosina to remain near the railing so she would be a part of the shots he would take from that higher elevation. When, some weeks hence, he was to view the blue-green slides, he could hardly find her amid a dozen gay-colored sun-umbrellas projecting like giant lollipops against the distant lake. But, he would remember that they had eaten lunch at a table beneath the white one with blue octagonal circles, and she had worn a yellow dress.

Seated at that table, they found it impossible to concentrate on anything but the sweeping, romantic scenery. In the center, San Salvatore thrust his jagged peak upward in a bold bid for center stage.

"To look at," she pointed out to Ward, "this mountain is prettier than yours."

"That figures," he smiled. "You are prettier than I."

Disputing his simile, she laughed. "You do not look like that."

"If you turn your head sideways, it should remind you of my nose."

Involuntarily, she inclined her head, and they both burst into laughter.

How different it was, she reflected, to be here with him, compared to being alone on Sunday; only two days ago!

She smiled, and her eyes teased him. "After you climb up there to take your picture, if you are not too tired, we can go for a walk around the other side."

"I am sure I can stumble along," he said facetiously. "But if you suggest walking back down the mountain, and then back to Paradiso, … I draw the line!"

She led him to the chestnut tree where she had stood alone on Sunday. He took her in his arms.

"At last," he breathed, "I have been tormented by enforced distance long enough!"

She offered her lips willingly. He obliged with a kiss, warm and urgent, yet carefully controlled. After all, it was broad daylight. She drew away a little. He glanced at his watch.

"Two-thirty." he said. "It was two thirty when we arrived in Lugano, three days ago." She studied his face. "This is the half way point. In three more days I have to go back to Zürich."

"But," she calculated, "That is Friday."

"Right."

He observed perplexed dismay creep into her expression.

"Stan and I have a reservation at Schweitzerhof in Zürich for Friday night. We have to be at the airport by ten on Saturday morning."

She looked at the Alps, a million miles away.

"I'm staying…" she said in a flat voice, "… until Sunday."

An intolerable vision of saying good-bye on Friday forced a chill down Ward's spine. He pulled her close, holding her head against his neck. "Rosina, now that I have met you, I… don't want to… leave you."

One of us, she reasoned, has to face this sensibly. Bringing her hands up against his chest, she pushed away, then walked with heavy footsteps onward along the path.

"Tell her!" a voice from within, commanded. "Tell her you love her! Tell her now!"

He caught up to her and reached for her hands.

Her own inner voice warned, "smile, you little fool! Do not let him know… you care… that much!"

She turned, forced a warm smile, wrinkled her nose and said, "Come on, there are more trails to explore."

When the time is right, he mused, I will tell her.

"But," his inner thought prevailed, "You have only three days and three more nights. Only three!"

"Rosina?"

"Yes?"

"After dinner tonight, would you like to ride out on the lake?" He had a vision of a darkened boat gliding across moonlit water, holding her close, feeling her hair against his neck.

"Yes, Ward, that would be… nice." Her vision conjured up a magical, moonlight sail. Another journey into delightful unreality.

* * *

Late that night, Ward knocked discreetly on his hotel room door. No answer or sound came from within, so he used his key and entered. Without turning on lights, he walked through the room and stepped onto his balcony. A streak of moonlight glistened across blue-black water: the same water he and Rosina had cruised on earlier, aboard a sleek white steamer. At Caprino, they had disembarked for open-air dancing. There had been little conversation during the entire excursion.

Later, as the boat docked at Paradiso landing, she had said, "And now, back to Paradiso."

"I have been in Paradise all evening," he had answered. Everywhere here, is paradise, not just this strip!"

"Yes," she agreed, "It is."

"I will hate to leave it, when the time comes," he said, in a tone of resigned sadness.

"Do not talk about it, … I do not like to think of it."

"But…."

"No, please," she begged.

They had stopped beside the red bench. He recalled pulling her down beside him.

"Tell me about the United States… where you live, and also… about your family."

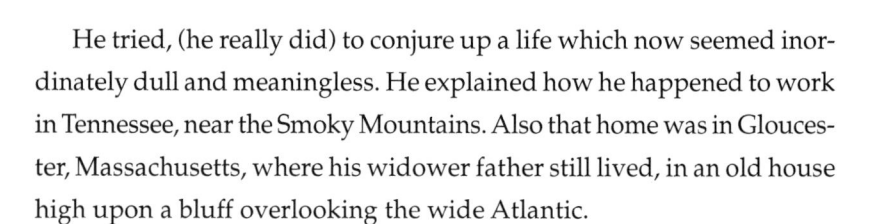

He tried, (he really did) to conjure up a life which now seemed inordinately dull and meaningless. He explained how he happened to work in Tennessee, near the Smoky Mountains. Also that home was in Gloucester, Massachusetts, where his widower father still lived, in an old house high upon a bluff overlooking the wide Atlantic.

"I have never seen the ocean."

"No, I suppose you haven't."

"Did you say that your father lives… all alone?"

"Sure, he likes it that way. My sisters live in Gloucester too, in homes of their own. In fact, my sister Jean, her husband Cass, and their three kids live right next door. Dad likes kids, but he says he will keep on liking them if they are not under foot all the time."

"Your mother?"

"Mom died five years ago."

"Oh," She paused, and he wondered what she was thinking. "How far away from him is Tennessee?"

"More than a thousand miles."

"A thousand miles sounds like… a long way."

"Yes, about four times the distance across Switzerland."

"How often do you see him?"

"I fly up every Christmas. Drive up for two weeks every summer. I know what you're thinking, Rosina, but I live my life and Dad lives his."

"He must be… rather lonely… living like that."

"Well now, he's not really alone. He's got Anne Carter, his housekeeper. And one of these days he'll realize that he can't get along without her and then… he will probably marry her."

"Do you have a house in Tennessee?"

"No, an apartment."

"And you have… a girlfriend, a fiancee?"

"At the moment, no. But tell me. Why do you want to know… these things?"

"When you are gone, I will have something to think about. I will get a map and...."

Taking hold of her chin, he turned her face up to his.

"Do I mean that much to you?"

Without flinching, she responded, "Yes."

"You are very candid, Rosina."

"Candid?"

"You say... exactly what you think."

"I only do, what comes natural to me."

He kissed her with great ardour... for a full minute.

"That comes natural to you?"

Her eyelids dropped. Breathlessly, she answered, "Yes."

"What about when Karl kisses you?"

She stiffened. "I have no affection for Karl."

"But you do... for me?"

"It is cold out here. I think we should say good-night. I do not like this conversation."

"We'll go in a minute. There is something I want you to understand. If I had met you at home somewhere, we would have time; like weeks or months, to get better acquainted. But this... six days! ... is so little time! Do you understand what I am trying to say?"

"Yes. I understand." She stood up. "We must go in."

Now he heard Stan turn his key. The door opened. A light flicked on. Ward walked back inside—glancing at Stan's mussed bed. "Looks like you had a good time."

"Sure did. I've heard about Swedish girls, but, " he exclaimed with delighted self-satisfaction, "they've got nothing on the Dutch."

"Like putty in your hands, huh?"

"Um, um," he answered with feeling. He removed his coat and hung it in the closet. "Thanks for staying out so late."

"No trouble at all. I was pleasantly... occupied."

"You were, huh?" Stan raised a knowing eyebrow at Ward, then walked into the bathroom and snapped on a light. "Kinda nice, your Swiss girl having her own room." He turned on cold water, reached for his toothbrush.

Ward lit his pipe, blew out the match. " It makes no difference… I have never been in her room."

A surprised Stanley stopped squirting toothpaste on his brush and stared wide eyed at his reflection. He blinked, then turned around and came back into the room.

Ward sat in a chair, untying a shoe with his free hand.

A sympathetic Stanley blurted out, "You mean… she's a cold fish!"

Ward straightened up, drew on his pipe. "No, I wouldn't say that." He remembered her warmth, her vital response, her careless abandon. It was he who kept their emotions controlled, not her. To Stan, he spoke with conviction, "I want her for the rest of my life… not just a few nights!"

Quite bewildered Stan went back into the bathroom. He certainly did not understand why one could not have both.

Later, in a darkened room, each lying in his own bed, Stanley asked, "You've kissed her?"

"Of course, many times."

"Propose to her?"

"That's the hell of it Stan. How do you propose to a girl, four days after you meet her?"

"Easy, I love you. Will you marry me?"

"For me, marriage means… a lifetime."

"Hmn, well, it's your life. But Christ, if I were you, I'd be climbing the walls by now!"

"And you… think, I'm not?"

"I think… you're nuts!, not doing anything about it."

Chapter Nine

On Wednesday morning a half-wakened girl rolled over in bed to reach an incessant ringing telephone. "Rosina, here," she droned into the instrument.

"I have awakened you." Ward spoke intimately. "Sleepy head."

"What time is it?" She glanced at drawn drapes which kept her room dark.

"Eight-thirty, but don't bother to get up. It is raining."

"Oh yes, I hear tires on the pavement."

"No concert this morning."

"It will be inside, in the Casino."

"How did you know that?"

"It is printed on the program."

"I can't read Italian."

"It is also printed in German, French, and English," she admonished. "You are not very observing!"

"That's not so!" he contradicted. "I *am* observing. I can see that you have gorgeous blue eyes, lovely brown hair, a beautiful figure, and luscious warm lips...."

"Ward!" she cautioned, "On the telephone!"

"I'll be right down, if you'd rather I tell you in person."

"No!" she answered with vehemence, as she swung up to a sitting position, and glanced down at mussed pink pajamas.

He laughed at her obvious discomposure. "Seriously, my darling, sleepy girl, take your time getting up. I have some shopping to do. Will you meet me at the Casino a little before eleven?"

"Yes."

At five before eleven, she stood in the salon entrance watching him cross the foyer toward her.—A moment in time, which turns expectancy to joy.—How delightful it was, to have met such a charming companion. Her secret thought came sparkling forth in the warm smile she gave him.

"Good morning, sleepy head, " he responded.

"You kept me up late last night."

"And I will, tonight, tomorrow night, and...."

She cut him off, "I have a table reserved for us, come."

He followed as she threaded her way between crowded tables. From the left corner, musical instruments squawked monotonous, discordant A's. He held her chair, catching a glimpse of sun-tanned thighs as a short blue skirt became even shorter in a sitting position.

"You have not worn that dress before, " he said, appraising the rest of it above the table, as he sat down beside her. How nice, he thought, that everything she wears accents her body. He suffered an instant vision of faded dungarees, sloppy shirts, and tent-like shawls parading down every city street in the U.S.A.

"I thought men did not... notice what women wore."

"You forget," he gave her a penetrating look. "I am observant."

Rosina changed the subject. "Did you complete your shopping?"

He laid down a package, too large for his pocket. "Yes, I bought six automobiles."

"Six?" She read the name, "Franz Karl Weber", on the package.

"Sure, for three nephews; two apiece."

"I could have gone with you... to buy toys."

"Not on your life!" he said, to cover the fact that he also went to a jewelers. "I wouldn't take a chance on your thinking I had three sons!"

She shot him a sideways glance of deep chagrin.

In that moment the conductor circled his way around violins and stepped up to his place, cognizant of his focal position. Respectful applause snapped throughout the hall. He turned, bowed, turned back again, and raised poised hands to launch his alert musicians into Rossini's "Tancredi Overture".

Rosina and Ward relaxed in rapt attention.

Tonight, he thought, I'll ask her to wear that frilly, green dress. It will make a better back-drop than peach for a green jade ring. He glanced down at a loose strand of brown hair which looped across peach colored skin, ending beside full sensuous lips. She reached fingers across her forehead, to push it back. He felt a great swelling within his chest, thinking, "tonight I will ask her to marry me."

By late afternoon skies had cleared, leaving a clear cool atmosphere which heightened the settling sunlight into yellow brilliance. Ward and Rosina walked southward along the highway carved out of Monte San Salvatore's steepest side. The road led up-hill to the headland of San Martino.

Ward sensed unusual preoccupation in Rosina ever since she had come downstairs that evening. After dinner he had asked what she would like to do and received a vague, "… to walk on and on… into the setting sun." Thus they walked. On top of the rise, at a curved lookout, they stopped to admire a sweeping panorama.

All evening, Rosina had tried to not think about her two phone calls, hating the reality which forced it's pre-eminence into her present dream world. (For wasn't this what she had now? A dream world, in this lovely Holiday… in Paradise?) As promised, she had telephoned home, and was told to call Karl. Vati had not given out information, he had only promised to convey Karl's message. She called Basel.

"Liebling " cried a frantic Karl Niederer. "Where are you?"

"On holiday," she answered with more patience than she felt.

"Yes, of course, but where?"

"I would rather _not_ tell you," she answered stiffly. "On Sunday, I have a reservation on the T.E.E. (Trans European Express) leaving at nine. If you wish, you may meet me in Zürlch. It should arrive about noon."

"Three hours? You are south, near Italy!"

"Forget it Karl, just meet me on Sunday."

"You are in Locarno. I'll bet you are!"

"No, not Locarno."

"Lugano?"

"Karl, what possible difference does it make?"

"Because, I am coming down!."

Oh, God in heaven, she thought, trying to maintain a calmness she did not feel. "No Karl, I am resting, relaxing, and thinking."

"I will not prevent you from resting, relaxing and thinking," he cajoled. "Please let me come?"

She felt cruel to refuse a, "Please".

"Wh… when would you want to… come?"

"I would drive down Friday, then we could come back together on Sunday."

"What time Friday?"

"I have to be in Zürich Friday, but I could get away by sixteen hours, and arrive in Lugano about twenty."

She thought about it. Ward was leaving at seventeen hours. No, it was too close. She could not cope with it.

"Rosina?"

"I am here. I am thinking. "

"Well? "

"If you will not come until Saturday morning, I will tell you where I am."

"All right, Saturday morning."

"Promise?"

"I promise."

Ward interrupted her thinking. "You have been staring at Monte Brè for a long time, Rosina, but you are not really seeing it, are you?"

"What? Oh, Monte Brè, yes," she flustered.

"You are troubled by something. What is it?"

Even though she wore a sweater, a chill shook her.

Ward moved to put his arm around her. "You are actually shivering, my darling. Are you that cold?"

"It is breezy here. And warmth is leaving with the sun. I will be all right if we start walking again."

"Then let's go back."

From the south a shrill whistle piped. She turned to see a train speed across the trestle from Switzerland into Italy. She hesitated long enough to watch it disappear. The weird shriek—echoing through her brain—caused her to snuggle against the muscular chest beside her. "Ward," she whispered, "Hold me close."

His other arm swept around her—and with a firm hand—pressed her head protectively against his shoulder. His lips spoke through the delightful softness of her hair. "Any time, my darling, for all time, forever and ever."

Oh God! she thought. If only it could be... forever!

Twin tears escaped her eyelids which she bravely checked by taking a deep breath. " I am all right now, thank you. Let's go back."

At the bottom of the hill, Ward stopped beside brightly lit Hotel Eden. "It is too cold for you to stay outside. Shall we go in here for coffee, or a drink?"

"No!" she answered sharply. "I would rather go back to our hotel."

Her decisiveness surprised him. His intention had only been to offer a new surrounding.

She noticed his frown, and said. "I feel more at home, at Beau Rivage, " But what she thought was how, when Karl had asked the name of her hotel, she had said Eden, because she did not want him in the same one with her.

As Ward led her across the street into a now familiar driveway, she felt—with certainty—that Karl would not confirm lt, either with the hotel, or with Vati. Why should he? He had what he wanted. And by Saturday night she would be too numb to care.

They found a table in the bar. Ward ordered drinks.

"I hope this makes you feel better," he said, raising his glass—perceiving at once the gravity in her eyes.

"Oh, I am fine now," she answered, forcing a brave smile.

He leaned back and studied her with solemn intensity. Something of enormous magnitude disturbed her. How best, he wondered, could he offer reassurance?

She turned away to gaze at a barely visible Monte Brè. Some of its lights twinkled through palm trees and around the heads of other people. Quiet chatter, occasional laughter, a clinking swish of ice against a cocktail shaker, instilled in her a sudden comparison. The difference between this resort bar, sitting beside a quiet, thoughtful, deeply considerate man; to the noisy, song-filled, beer flowing places where she went with 'happy-go-lucky' Karl.

One memory with Karl came vividly alive. They had gone to Oepfelkammer, in old Zürich's eastern quarter. Seated in the rear—a party of five—two men and three girls commandeered attention. One played guitar. Everyone sang. Smoky air stung Rosina's eyes and nostrils. The golden, foamy beer so repelled her that Karl drank both his own and hers. The odd girl flirted outrageously with Karl and he had no objection when Rosina asked to leave. At the bottom of the stairs, she realized Karl was not directly behind. In a moment he came bounding down the worn, stone steps. It took only ten minutes to drive her home. That particular affair lasted two months. She knew about lt. Karl made certain of that. He also knew she would make excuses to her parents. They were realists. They would merely have said, "Well, what do you expect?"

She felt time slipping away—ticking off minutes, hours, nights. Only two more <u>nights!</u> She made an impulsive decision.

"When we finish these, let's go up to my room…" She hesitated, "…the view is better."

She sensed his eyes studying her face, which told him nothing—for a profile rarely transmits one's inner feelings. But all the same, her jaw trembled and pin pricks stung her entire body.

It was not late enough for moonlight when Ward followed her through a dark room toward the open balcony. Street lamps and auto headlight furnished enough glow to discern objects in the room. Rosina stopped at the open glass doors as Ward came behind, encircling both arms around her rib-cage. She felt the violent beating of his heart against her back and the light pressure of his lips on one side of her forehead.

He said, "I like this being able to leave doors and windows open with no insects coming in."

"Insects?"

"Sure, flies, moths, mosquitoes. At home, all doors and windows are screened to keep them out."

"Everywhere in the United States?"

"Every place I have been."

"I do not think screens are necessary anywhere in Switzerland."

"Which is just one more of its inestimable qualities."

She felt his heart gradually slow its pace. She wondered about a country which had to screen out insects.

"Last night," he began, hoping to get her talking, "I told you about my life. Now suppose you tell me about yours?"

"I have already told you."

"There has to be more to your life than a dictator father and the fair-haired grocery boy!"

She chuckled. He certainly had a way of reducing everything to a common denominator. It was utterly superfluous to state that Karl had jet-black hair.

"Besides being an efficient secretary, what else can you do? For instance, do you like to ski?"

"Yes." She had never been skiing except with Karl. "Yes," she repeated. "I like to ski."

"Hmn. How about those bad habits of yours?"

She sighed. "Well, for one thing, I am… sometimes rude to people I do not like. Immediately afterward, I am sorry."

"We shall work on that. Right now I am more concerned with whether you leave the cap off the toothpaste or wear curlers to bed?"

She tried to turn around, but his grip held her tight.

"Another question, can you cook? I do like to eat."

With the force of both her hands over his, she twisted around to face him. "Can I cook?" she mocked. "Of course I can. All Swiss women can cook!"

"That's good." he said, pulling her head close beside his and whispering Into her ear. "Will you marry me?"

"Marry you!" Her own voice startled her.

"Yes, marry me, come to the United States with me?"

Myriad conflicts flashed behind her closed eyes, which transfused her into stunned silence. This was a possibility so remote she had not—even once—considered it.

Ward relaxed his hold upon her head—waiting with bated Brèath for an answer.

Had he been truly serious, or did he tease her still? She looked up, "Why? Because I would not wear curlers to bed, or because I can cook?"

"Neither. I want to marry you, because I love you."

He bent to kiss her. She felt warm lips press onto hers with definite urgency. Lost in a whirlwind of frightening indecision, she could not immediately respond, but soon found it impossible to do otherwise. He held her locked so close she abandoned all reason and pressed her hands across his back. There was no restraint in him. His mouth bore hard against hers. And she, carried by the unrelenting violence of such impact—returned in kind exactly what he gave. Waves of unexplainable, unendurable desire spread throughout her body. She wanted to stop—to regain some stability—but, oh! oh! oh! she wanted even more fiercely, <u>not to</u>! Her breathing, became laborous. He pressed her so close against his body, she felt all of his masculine hardness. An involuntary, helpless cry came from inside her throat.

He released her slightly. Through deep, husky Brèaths, he whispered, " I want you, Rosina. I can't help it. I love you so much. Tell me… do you…?"

She laid her head against his chest, feeling a wildly beating heart thumping, beside her ear. Could the sublime fire within her be any less than that… within him?

With her arms still wrapped tightly around him, she did not let go. She wanted desperately for him to go on kissing her. "Oh Ward! I don't know what to say, or what to do… now." Tears flooded her eyes and a sob broke forth from deep inside. "Never… in my whole life… have I felt what I am feeling now."

"Don't cry about it, sweetheart."

He tried to lift her chin up, but she averted her face and burrowed against his chest. "I want…" she whispered huskily, "… whatever you want."

His hand caressed her hair. "First things first, Rosina. You haven't answered my question. Will you marry me?"

She opened her eyes to see only a blur of green chiffon pressed against a white shirt. "I cannot."

"Cannot? Why can't you?"

"I told you. My life is here in Switzerland. I can do nothing to change that." Intense pathos retracted tight furrows between her eyebrows. "I have not misled you into believing otherwise."

"No, you haven't." He stared intently down into her eyes. "Now tell me that you do <u>not</u> love me."

"I… I," she faltered, buckling under his intense gaze.

"Look at me."

"Oh, what is the use?" she cried. "Even if I tell you that I love you, I still cannot marry you."

He dropped his arms with such abruptness, she nearly lost her balance. Angrily, he spoke to her "Of all the pig headed, stubborn females I have ever known, you are the worst!" Had he emptied a bucket of ice water on her, the shock would have been no different.

"Ward, please," she begged. Both her hands gripped each side of his waist. "I do love you... you know that without making me say it."

"Yes, I know." He placed his hands to frame her face. His thumbs felt her trembling jaw; his fingers, the pulse beating ln her neck. "But," he added with a sick empty feeling, "... not enough."

At this accusation she burst into tears, her whole body seemed to be awash with them.

He held her until the storm subsided. Then, despite the constricting band of torment in his own throat, he managed to say "Since you have made up your mind, there is no point in my staying. I had better go."

A sense of alarm widened her tear-stained eyes. "I do not want you to... leave." Her eyelids dropped, "I w... want you to... stay."

"No! I'm too angry!"

"Would you please listen to my side of it?"

Impatience rose within him. "Your side!"

She saw his eyes flash as they had the day he bought the blouses. "You are stubborn too. You won't even let me explain!"

With reluctant steps, he walked over to a chair and slumped into it.

Rosina moved behind it. She laid one hand on his shoulder, the other, on his hair. " I never knew," she spoke with plaintive sadness, "that I would love... and be loved like this. Every girl dreams of fairy-tale romance; the charming prince; the far away castle. A long time ago, I faced the fact that for me, it is only that, a dream."

Ward reached up to hold the hand upon his shoulder, while Rosina threaded nervous fingers through his hair.

"I have been brought up to be a dutiful daughter. Respect for—and strict obedience to—my parents' wishes, dominates my thinking. Whether or not I marry Karl, I could not... condemn my parents to life without me."

A tear dropped on Ward's hand. He sprang to his feet and drew her into his arms, tenderly kissing her wet eyelids, then burning cheeks and finally her trembling lips.

"Rosina, Rosina. Every woman, since the beginning of time has faced the fact that—no matter how painful it is—she must cut parental ties. I'm not asking you to never see them again. The United States is only seven hours from here by plane. "

When she did not answer, he went on, "I realize this is all rather sudden, but I find it difficult to believe that... you won't even consider it. You are no longer a child. Stop thinking like one!"

"Oh Ward, you just don't understand!"

He released her as quickly as though she had become a hundred pound cake of ice. "You're damned right! I don't understand!" He moved away—toward the door. After a few steps—and with his back toward her—he spoke in toneless accusation.

"There is something else I don't understand." He felt as bereft as on the day his mother died. "... how you could... allow me to make love to you—as I surely would have—knowing that... you would never see me again."

It would have been unbearable—in that moment—to look upon her face. He opened the door, moved outside, then closed it quietly behind him.

The lock clicked. She felt the sound vibrate in her limp arms. She ran to throw herself across the bed. Racking sobs came from deep inside her chest. In her brain, the sound of her own crying mingled with that of the ticking clock. My God! What have I done? What am I doing? to him, and to myself? How empty the room had become! Just as empty, she thought, as my life will be, after he has gone... forever!

She placed both elbows on the spread, and propped her chin upon two palms. She began to think of how she might work it out. I will explain to Mutti, and she will help me tell Vati. She shuddered, and tried again. Jeanette will help me tell Mutti, then together... Oh Gott in Himmell! ... Vati hates Jeanette!

"You are no longer a child, stop thinking like one!" rang repeatedly in her ear.

Sobered by the memory of his words, she got to her feet. Undoing the back zipper, she slipped out of the green dress. Before hanging it in the closet, her eyes studied it with sad recollection. "Why is it, that things always happen differently from the way you expect them to?"

At the lift, Ward hesitated before pushing the up button, to look at his watch. Dammit, only eleven! He went down instead, into the bar.

After his second drink, he casually reached into his pocket, where his hand gripped a small box. Why in hell, he thought, can't things work out the way you want them to?"

He paid his check, then went over to the house phone. No answer from Stanley.

He went up to bed—drifting immediately into a dead sleep. But into his dormant mind crept a tormenting dream. Switzerland was no longer beautiful. It was a great dark prison. One which kept Rosina in and himself out. Repeatedly he reached out to grasp her, but monstrous hands held her beyond his reach. Frustrated by the effort, he seemed to stand helplessly by as she pummeled away—as though from some high pinnacle—falling end over end, like a maple seed, around and around, down into a never-ending vortex—her voice echoing with ringing reverberation, "Ward... Ward... Ward... Ward...."

Three floors below, the object of his nightmare found no relief in sleep. At first she lay on her back staring wide-eyed into the vacuous dark. Hating the blankness of it she closed her eyes... tight! Layers of her body seemed to peel away; her skin, her muscles, her face... leaving only bones—pulled in one direction, then another, as though they were made of rubber. She turned over, buried her face in a pillow—

already wet with tears—and vainly wished for the blessed oblivion of sleep. After endless hours of such torment, she got out of bed, put on a robe, and strode out onto the balcony. A shimmering shaft of moonlight glistened on a melancholic lake. So violent was a pressing ache within her head that the silvery shaft appeared like a cold glacier vacillating slowly toward her heart.

She went back inside, into the bathroom, turned on the light, filled a glass with water, and swallowed two aspirin.

Before she crawled back under the sheet, she stared apathetically at the bed-side phone. She could pick it up… could talk to Ward. Perhaps then, some of the agony would lessen. But the luminous hands of her travel-clock said no, for they both pointed to three.

She curled up on her side, pulling covers over her head, waiting for knots in her stomach to stop wrenching her heart. It was not frustration which nagged her now, it was guilt! The truth of it so repellent, she kept pushing it back in her mind—trying to replace it with more pleasant thoughts. But the black clouds of conscience forced her to face the truth of Ward's parting words. He had accused her of being no better than a… Schlampe! She could not recall its English translation—if indeed she had ever learned it. Self-accusation pounded hatefully inside her mind. "You thought you could play a game with your emotion! Thought you could experience the deepest ecstasy of love, then calmly say, "Goodbye. It was nice knowing you."

She felt sick with revulsion.

Of all the indignities in our lives—she admonished herself—those we perpetrate against ourselves, are the very worst.

Chapter Ten

Toward morning Rosina fell asleep. For quite suddenly she awoke to hear a phone ringing with repeated insistence. As she picked it up, her eyes opened to sunlight boldly dominating the opposite wall. "Rosina Wyler, here."

A harsh, masculine voice—cold and derisive—came through the instrument. "I am ready for Breakfast. I expect you to join me."

"I am still in bed."

"I will wait."

"It would be better not to. I..." she hesitated, "... I am not hungry."

"Hungry or not, I expect you downstairs... in half an hour."

"No,"

"You will find me on the terrace. Good-bye."

She stared with stupefied wonder at the now dead telephone, then spoke to it as though it were not some inanimate object. "I cannot imagine him wheedling me with '<u>Please</u> let me come to Lugano'."

She wore the blue dress, and made it to the terrace exactly five minutes later than the prescribed half-hour.

She stared at two pitchers, one of hot coffee; the other of hot milk; just the way she liked it! Ward had already ordered for her. He <u>knew</u> she would come! Knew it as an absolute fact! She stared into his blue—coldly piercing—eyes. Her unsmiling mouth hung open.

"You see now, don't you, that whatever anyone tells you to do, you do it... automatically! Just like a robot."

She stared through tired, stinging eyelids, digesting the truth of what he said.

"Unless you learn—in the chess game of life—to stand up confidently, and be the queen that you are... instead of a pawn, you will never reach your full capacity of a woman." He broke open a roll and reached for some butter.

"Are you finished, Doctor Freud?" she asked—with biting sarcasm.

"For the moment. Now drink your coffee!"

"No! I refuse," she answered.

A sardonic smile crept across his face. "I do believe there is hope for you yet."

As she poured the coffee and milk into her cup, he asked, "Did you look at your eyes this morning?"

"You did not give me time."

"Fine thing. I propose to a girl and she spends the night crying."

Irritated by the lack of empathy, she retorted, "I suppose you slept easily?." She sipped her coffee.

"Like a log, he answered. Then added, "with the help of two more drinks at the bar."

"After you... left me?"

"Sure." he said with a rueful grin. Then, drawing a brochure of Lugano from his pocket, he continued. "There are a lot of places I have not seen yet, so let's get on with them. First there is, "Santa Maria degli An-gi-o-li." (She repressed a desire to correct his pronunciation.) "It states, 'Crucifixion' by Luini. After that I'd like to see these other Cathedrals and this Art gallery.

"Apparently, today I must do what you want."

"Right! This is your country and I am the tourist. Furthermore, I need a guide. Now eat your rolls."

"What about the concert? Are we to miss that?"

The way she said it reminded him of Debbie asking for an ice-cream cone. "We'll go to the concert. It is one thing we both enjoy. If you were not behaving like a… moron, you would realize we could have a whole lifetime of enjoying things together."

She bristled. "Isn't a moron someone of little intelligence?"

"You are so right! In fact you amaze me. "Most of the time your grasp of English is clear as a crystal glass. But the meaning of three simple words like, I love you, is no clearer to you than a night of dense fog."

With chilling resentment, she fired back. "I'll bet that when you were a boy, you were mean to animals!"

"Well, now, if you care to discuss meanness, suppose you consider, seriously, what you are doing to me."

The fierceness of his accusation unnerved her. If only she could reach over and touch him and say, "I'm sorry." But that alone would not suffice. He wanted but one word from her. And that word was… yes.

His eyes still bored into her. "Oh, I've suffered before in my life," he went on, "One time—skiing—I broke my leg. It was wrenched and twisted beneath me. I could bear the excruciating pain, knowing that within hours it would be fixed. But the pain you have inflicted on me… will last a hell of a lot longer than that."

She lowered her eyes to a half-empty cup. He knew by her anguished expression the barb had hit its mark. He did not intend to goad her too far, but neither did he intend to let her off easily. He reached into his pocket.

"Rosina. Let's not spend our last day together by arguing." He passed a small white box across the table. "Here is something I intended to give you last night."

She looked down at the tiny box he had placed in her hand, then lifted questioning eyes to his.

"It is something to remind you of your favorite mountain." he said.

Inadvertently she raised her eyes to look across the lake. In hardly more than a whisper, she asked, "Brè?"

"Humph. It surely isn't Salvatore!"

She snapped open the box and stared hard at the ring inside; A perfectly rounded cone of cobalt blue encased by etched leaves of yellow gold.

"Did you know,"—he relayed information from the jeweler—"... that emeralds are only cut in squares and rectangles?"

"Ward! I cannot accept this!"

"I see that I am still dealing with Rosina the pawn," he sighed. "A queen would simply say, 'thank you'."

She slipped the ring upon her finger and—though she smiled through tear-filled eyes—he noted that some of the agony had left her face.

"Thank you, Ward. I do like it."

"Now we are making progress!" he announced with satisfaction. Secure in the knowledge that he had succeeded in making her quite miserable he determined to spend the next few hours... making her happy.

During the entire day of sightseeing, neither of them mentioned that which clouded their separate minds, the horrendous aspect of the previous night.

At five thirty they returned to the hotel. A foot weary Rosina stepped ahead of Ward into the lift.

"I hope you do not want to go dancing tonight; I can hardly walk."

"After a quick swim you'll be refreshed. Tonight," he said, decisively, "we are going to Campione."

"And what is at Campione?"

The door opened on three. They stepped out into the hall. Ward produced two white cards from an inside pocket and passed them to Rosina. She read; Casino Municipal de Campione, Carte d'Entree. On one: delivree a Mademoiselle R. Wyler. The other: delivree a Monsieur W. Fairbanks. Stamped in blue across the bottom: Hotel Beau Rivage. She passed them back.

"The boat leaves at nine. Now go get your swimsuit on."

"I might not <u>want</u> to go swimming," she challenged.

"Well I do. And you are going with me."

He pushed the up button. The door immediately reopened. "When," she asked. "Did you get the entry cards?"

He stepped inside. "This morning before you came down for Brèakfast." The lift door slid shut between them.

A few minutes later—inside her room—she stared at a vase upon the dresser, out of which protruded… a dozen dark red roses.

That night, shortly after nine, a white pleasure steamer—proudly wearing a red and white shield upon her bow—churned up to Debarcadero in Paradiso. More than twenty people moved up the ramp to merge with a chattering throng already aboard. A gate slammed shut behind them. The ship's propellers swished and chugged, then gracefully, they pushed it outward on calm blue water. Ward and Rosina found seats near the forward rail. Deck lights dimmed and a round orange moon peeked over San Salvatore. Ward's left arm encircled Rosina, whose head lay against his shoulder. For several minutes they sat in silence, watching dark Italian mountains looming up ahead. Each hid from the other a wish to suspend time—to hold back the night—to block sand from flowing through an hour-glass—on this, their last evening in Lugano. Neither dared put into words the frightening finality which bore wretchedly onward with every pulsation of the ship's engine. She had not thanked him for the roses. She chose this moment to do so, then asked, "How you possibly managed it when I was with you all day…?"

"It's like this. Once there lived a man named Alexander Graham Bell.…"

"Oh Ward! How can you make fun when we are both so… so miserable?"

Instead of answering, he reached for her hand. His thumb touched the ring he had given her. "Do you really like it?"

"Yes, very much."

"You <u>are</u> going to keep it?"

"Yes."

"And wear it?"

"Yes. Although I do not know how… I will have to explain it."

Before he could ask the <u>necessity</u> of explaining it to anyone, the boat had docked at Campione. Music—which had drifted out across the shimmering water—had become loud and gay. Tiny squares of light had enlarged into huge windows of brightness. A carnival atmosphere—enhanced by colored lanterns—prevailed upon the scene.

Several passengers—besides Ward and Rosina—disembarked to stroll upward, across a bridge into the Casino. Behind them, the boat dimmed her lights and slipped off to seek another shore.

"Ward," she whispered with alarm, "This is Italy! I do not have a passport."

"I doubt if we'll be asked. If so, say that you left it in your room. The entrance cards should be enough."

As Ward predicted, an attendant merely looked at the cards.

At first Ward and Rosina watched men and women gambling at roulette, then strolled further on to watch Baccarat players.

"I suppose you are used to this sort of thing?" he asked.

"No. We have gambling in some cities, but not for such high stakes."

Arm in arm, they walked down broad stairs into a large salon. A waiter led them to a table which Ward specified as; "Some distance from the orchestra, please." He could not talk to her with horns blasting in their ears.

He ordered Champagne. When the bottle arrived and was opened with a foaming "pop", Rosina watched in fascination while the waiter filled two crystal glasses.

Then Ward held his glass up to hers, clinking the edge.

"To a beautiful companion who has given me a truly memorable week."

She touched the glass to her lips. Over the curved rim she studied his face with deep intensity. Bubbles stung her tongue. "It sounds so… final."

"You have made it final," he accused.

Considerably shaken, she drank more, for it eased her dry throat. From the orchestra—at that moment—came melancholy strains of a classically familiar melody; "September Song." Like a bell jangling a vibrant nerve she felt her heart turn over.

Automatically, Ward stood up, took her hand and led her to the dance floor—for he loved to dance with her.

In his arms she began to sing in soft tones; "Oh it's a long—long—time,—from—May—to…" But a choking sob welled in her throat and the notes for "December" formed only in her brain. Tears escaped from stinging eyes to course `down across her burning cheeks onto Ward's beige jacket so very near her face. She tightened her right hand in his and pressed tense fingers of the other upon his shoulder.

He sensed the desperation within her—which he knew came from the rough moments he gave her—but this was not the moment to slacken. He had suffered as much because of her, as he now did for her. And it would have been small comfort to know which facet of their situation bugged her at this particular instant; the bitter words of last night or the inevitableness of parting on the morrow. Instead of asking, he spoke with casual nonchalance, like one discussing the weather.

"I was born in September."

"Me too…."

"Which day?"

"Tenth."

"Mine is the seventh." Silently then, he guided her around other couples—holding her too close to see her haunting look of despair.

At the song's conclusion, final words drummed inside her brain.

"… these precious days… I'll spend with you."

Rosina stopped abruptly. Moving away from him, she turned to thread her way—almost running—back toward their table. Ward—directly behind—arrived in time to hold her chair.

She sat down, picked up an almost empty glass, drained it, set it down, leaving her thumb and forefinger pressed across its base. She studied a bubbling stream as Ward refilled it. With sudden realization, that it was not her feet which were tired, but her head, she blinked, trying to focus on, two? ... three? ... No! only one glass of bubbles.

The song's symbolic words had also reached Ward. Lest his voice betray him, he spoke gruffly.

"Drink your champagne."

Suddenly, she snapped her head in the direction of his voice. Anger flamed in her eyes. "You have been giving me orders all day!"

"Well," he grinned with smug relief, "I thought you'd never notice!"

Stunned for only a second, she spoke in solemn wonder.

"You... have done it... on purpose!"

"Of course. Goading you constantly, I wondered how much you'd take before you fought back. You have become so accustomed to it, you don't know the difference. You remind me of a puppy who, when his leash is unhooked, romps away in great delight, but comes running back when he hears that whistle. Your mother and father won't always be around to blow that whistle, Rosina, or clip on that leash."

She swallowed, but the lump in her throat refused to budge. She recalled other words he had said last night, "Pig-headed, stubborn!" and this morning at Brèakfast, "a pawn!" She drew a long Brèath,—to stay the fear and nausea pressing icy currents into her flushed body. Her gaze held fast against Ward's eyes, which burned into her very soul. A picture of servile existence flashed behind her. An unknown future stretched ahead. Bleak or exciting? Dull or full? Subservient or independent? A pawn or a... queen? Ward forced her to realize that what she held as agreement, because she loved her parents, was instead... appeasement!

Ward,—in expressing his love,—offered her freedom. Could she take it? Simply reach out to him and accept it? Her hand reached up to touch his cheek. The tenseness there, eased. A trace of smile parted his lips before he shifted them to kiss the palm of her hand.

With the brief caress, came a flood of memory for... last evening! She now wished, with all her heart, that it could somehow, be erased. She looked down, away from his hypnotic eyes to tiny sword and shield motifs on a brown necktie.

"I am sorry about last night," she said.

"So am I, but it was as much my fault as yours."

"What I mean is... I would have... I almost...." The words came hard.

He recalled his dream, seeing her at some unobtainable distance. He had to reach out.

"I know what you are trying to say."

She lifted pained, inquiring eyes to his.

"You offered your heart... and body, like a Vestal Virgin on a sacrificial altar. Your common sense, was neatly tucked away... somewhere else!"

The words stung, as he meant they should.

"I am so ashamed."

"You don't need to be."

He leaned closer and clasped her hand between both his own. So near were his eyes that she could not look at both of them at once, but had to focus from one to the other.

"It was not easy for me to... leave you last night." He paused, choosing his words with care. "I am a selfish beast, Rosina. I want you... so very much, but I want <u>all</u> of you, or... nothing."

The waiter approached and laid a check on the table. "Signore, the last boat for Lugano, it leaves in ten minutes."

"Thank you," answered Ward. He laid a franc note over the check, reached for his glass, and drained it.

"Don't drink yours... unless you want to."

He spoke to a numb statue, whose eyes stared fixedly at the white tablecloth.

His whispered words drummed in her ears. "... all of you... I want all of you." Unaware of what she did, her hand picked up the tiny bowl of bubbles. Her lips moved automatically, as she sipped and sipped, until the glass was empty.

She stood up. Ward's reassuring hand slipped across her back, around her waist. As they skirted the dance floor, rhythmic drum-beats thumped against her head, and the room appeared filled with a million lights sparkling like stars in the Milky Way. She felt a firm grip on her arm. With no sense of her own direction, she was led out through the exit. Fresh, night air—like a slap across the cheek—stabilized her senses. She swallowed deep breaths of it. With mechanical steps, she walked along the ramp; wooden feet on a wooden platform. The music receded, further and further away.

Seated on the boat, Rosina lay her head against Ward's shoulder, closed her eyes, and fell asleep.

He looked down at the precious head in the crook of his right shoulder, and spread the fingers of his left hand through her hair, to press her even closer with tender protection.

During the twenty minute run to Paradiso, he spent about ten, wondering whether she had won or lost the battle raging within herself; About nine minutes visualising her in his apartment, then showing her off to his father, his sisters, his friends; And no longer than one—or possibly half a minute—did he give to the depressing thought of, <u>never seeing her again.</u>

The boat slowed. Lights brightened. Gently, Ward shook Rosina. "Wake up sweetheart."

Startled, she came to, shook her head, and looked up into Ward's eyes.

"I love you, Rosina."

"And I love you."

During the ten minute walk from the boat dock to the Beau Rivage Hotel, Rosina spoke not at all. Had she been spoken to, she could not have answered. Although she felt vague awareness that left foot followed right, one after the other, and that strong dependable arms guided her along the quay, across the street, and into the hotel, her mind had drifted onto a different scene.

She stood in the kitchen at home, facing her father. She did all of the talking. "Vati, in Lugano I met a man whom I love, who also loves me. As soon as I can arrange matters, I'm going to marry him. Please… do not interrupt! This man means everything to me. I want nothing in life so much, as I want to be with him… forever. No, father, he is not Swiss! Of course I will come back to see you. You will also come to visit me… Vati, I am truly sorry to disappoint you… about Karl. You must have known I never loved him."

Johann Wyler's arguments, weak and nebulous, barely infringed Rosina's soliloquy. It could not be otherwise, for this was her illusion, all of it went her way.

In the corridor, outside her door, Rosina placed her key in the lock.

Behind her, Ward studied the ravishing beauty of her disarranged hair… felt again the urge to run his fingers through its silken softness. Directly beyond her shoulder, a left hand pressed tense fingers upon the wooden door. It opened. Without turning she asked, "Will you come in?"

He wanted her with a desperate need. But he knew, that to possess her… for only one night, then say "good-bye" … forever! was more than he could endure. With unsteady voice, he whispered, "That depends…."

She stepped inside. He followed, closing the door behind him. A weird snap echoed in the silent room. Street traffic hummed from beyond the open balcony, and pale moonlight cast a shaft of light onto folds of golden drapes.

As she turned around to face him, his hands encased her waistline. In the semi-darkness, she lifted inquiring eyes to his.

"Depends, I suppose, on me."

"Yes, on whether you love me enough… to marry me?"

She ran fingers up along his cheek. "I want to, darling, believe me, I want to."

Ward detected the word "<u>but</u>" and chose to ignore it.

"How much do you want to?"

Her answer was a cry of pain. "With everything inside me, my heart, my blood, my whole being! I become terrified… at the thought of facing each day, knowing that you will be somewhere else in the world… wanting me as much as… I want you."

The power of her speech surged through him, yet its underlying tone gave no credence to her words. He spoke with stiffness. "What… are you going to do about it?"

She sighed with resignation. I will try to work it out, Ward. I want to marry you, but I need time."

His head moved from side to side. "That's not… enough!"

"Not…!" Rosina recoiled as though he had struck her, yet his hands had not moved from her waist.

"When will you realize that I am struggling with you, Rosina, not against an ingrained fear of leaving Switzerland, nor against your domineering father, or even against your inane obligation to both your parents! Don't you see, my precious girl, I am fighting against you! … against your inner self?"

Rosina trembled as she leaned toward him, and wrapped both arms across his back. His right arm drew her body close, the other pressed her head beneath his chin.

"Perhaps," he went on, "There is too great a difference in what I expect a woman… or at least my wife, to be, compared with… this old-world idea of male domination. It's important to me, that you stand on your own two feet. I want you to… accept me, all the way; no hesitation, no weakness, no wavering. Unless you have the courage to say, "This I believe, this I <u>will</u> do! regarding your future… our future, then it is better for us to part, now, before… we get further involved."

He held his breath, like one who plays an ace, and waits to be trumped.

To Rosina, all vacillation had come to an abrupt end. She had to face her conviction… now! She raised brave eyes which had filled with tears. Then, wrested from deep within her Brèast, came slow, tortured words.

"All right, Ward. I will marry you, no matter how it has to be done." She buried her face again in the shelter of his neck, and her voice became an agonized cry, "Because, I cannot live without you."

They kissed with love and passion which knew no restraint. Her quivering body, suppliant and yielding, urged him onward. Through demanding pressure of mouth and body, sprang a raging torrent which coursed through each blood-stream, and could no more be stopped than the river Reuss in its rampant fury—thundering over rocks and boulders—to splash with violent force… into the gorge below.

With one swift movement Ward released her, took off his jacket and tie, then removed his shoes which suddenly felt like two dead weights.

Rosina felt perspiration in her hands as she struggled to release the back zipper of her dress. She relaxed when Ward grasped the clasp, then slowly pulled it down the length of soft, fragile green. She stepped out of the dress and tossed it onto a chair.

He swept her up in strong arms and carried her to the bed. Then lying down—with his face above hers—he gazed into dark, rapturous eyes filled with strange wonder. Gently, his hand moved across her warm body as his lips kissed her forehead, her eyes, her cheek, her neck…, her breasts.

She felt hot, frightening waves of excitement carry her to a plain of absolute delight.

And when her hand moved beneath his shirt—lain tentative and tingling upon his bare flesh—he placed it where he wanted more vitally… to feel her touch.

And she—stunned by the pulse of life through that within her grasp—cried, "Oh Ward, I have never…."

Then before he consumed her lips entirely with his own, he answered with breathless tenderness, "I know, my love… I know."

Chapter Eleven

Shortly after eight on Friday morning, Rosina, wearing a yellow dress, stepped onto her balcony. Grasping the metal rail with both hands, she looked out across blue water into the morning haze surrounding Monte Brè, "Now I know," she whispered to herself, "why Karl wanted me so much." She breathed deeply of the warm air. "But, he wanted only, … to possess me, and I wanted… love.

Her gaze traveled downward until she observed, first a piece of red bench behind a clump of shrubs, then a gray flagstone path between red salvia borders, and nearby, a group of tall palm trees like inverted shaggy paint brushes, and close beneath her, jutting from the marquee, eleven assorted national flags lying limp in the quiet morning air.

Below the flags, a half circle of yellow sun umbrella reminded her that Ward probably sat beneath it waiting for her to join him.

She hurried back through her room, out the door, and down the corridor. Ignoring the lift, she ran down two stair flights, slowing her pace only when she approached people in the dining room. At the terrace doorway she saw him. With every fiber of her body tingling like a crescendo of sweeping harp glissandi, she moved toward him.

He stood up as she approached. His blue eyes sparkled with piercing intensity.

"The most thrilling sight I shall ever know, is of you, walking toward me." He said.

"It is rather nice for me too," she smiled, "To know… you are waiting."

Each studied the other's face as they sat down. Then Ward reached across the table to hold her hand.

"I find that I am at a loss for words this morning."

"It is something we don't need…" her eyelids lowered, "… to talk about." Then squeezing his hand, she quickly loosened its grip. "I'm hungry, and I need two hands to eat."

Ward watched those hands as she poured her coffee, buttered a roll, and bit off a large chunk. God! How he loved her!

He said, "We're going shopping this morning. I want to get my father a Swiss watch, and I need your advice about some jewelry for my sister. While we are there, I intend to buy… a wedding ring for you."

She finished chewing the roll in her mouth, then asked, as calmly as she might for another roll, "and for you…? I have noticed that American men wear rings, too?"

"Not for me, my dear. Sometimes I find it necessary to put on a hard hat and crawl around turbo-generators, have a conference in a machine shop, or meander beneath cranes and under pipes in nuclear stations we are building."

"B… but that could be dangerous!"

"Only if you don't duck, or carelessly put your hands where they don't belong."

"You must… travel a lot, in your work?"

"Mostly in Tennessee and North and South Carolina."

"Would you want me to… to go with you?"

"I surely will. Unless you get bored with it."

"Bored!" Her eyes opened incredibly wide. "… being with you? Oh my dear…."

Her response pleased him, but she had to know the score. "Many times I put in ten to fourteen-hour days."

"But not… the nights?"

"No, sweetheart." His face flashed s sensuous twinkle, "Not the nights."

"In that case," she agreed, reaching to butter another roll, "... I would go with you."

Ward decided on an abrupt end to this conversation, before the urge to take her upstairs got a further grip on him. "I canceled your room for tonight and Saturday. Your bill will be ready with ours."

The switch to the immediate present sobered Rosina. "I am going to pay my own hotel bill."

"If you wish. But I will not get on that train and leave you here. I want you with me as long as possible."

He recalled telling the manager that she had promised to marry him. "Ah that is good news M'sieur. I thought your reservations… a bit unusual… all made by Siegwart Freres, you all arrived together, yet <u>she</u> planned to stay through Sunday! Ah yes, M'sieur, I am happy for you."

A pained expression had formed around her eyes. "What time," she asked, "does the train leave?"

"At five this afternoon. We will have dinner on the way, and be in Zürich at eight-forty."

Silently, she poured more coffee and hot milk. He had not said Zürich any louder than the other words. It merely sounded louder, like it came out of a megaphone.

"Rosina?"

She looked up.

"You don't think I would let you face, Zürich, and your parents… alone?"

"They do not speak English, Ward."

"Then you can translate."

"I don't think…" her voice trailed off.

"You're forgetting something… I love you."

"I love you, too, " she answered, in a quiet, serious tone.

"Then let me do <u>some</u> of the thinking."

Five minutes before five, a sleek, red-engined train arrived from Milan. A half dozen north-bound passengers climbed aboard. Not many persons traveled north from Lugano at this hour on a Friday evening. More traveled south.

Rosina had a bad moment before boarding the train. On Thursday she had canceled her Sunday express reservation. While standing on the station platform, she suddenly remembered why! ... Karl!

She thought of phoning him, She had fifteen minutes.

"I would have to call the Zürich office. And what?" she pondered, "would I say to him?" Better to call later, in Zürich. He always stayed with Uncle Niclaus.

Ward and Rosina found the car with open seats instead of compartments. They seated themselves on one. Since no one occupied the seat in front, or behind, they might have been completely alone, except for Stanley, who moved in across the aisle.

"Sleep well last night?" Ward whispered into a bit of ear showing beneath auburn hair.

"Mm hum," she murmured. "I had a beautiful dream. You kissed my cheek and whispered, 'good-night, sleeping beauty'."

"That wasn't a dream."

"What time was it?"

"Three thirty."

"Is that when you left?"

"Uhn huh."

She snuggled against him. This morning when I awakened, my clothes were scattered... everywhere. I usually hang them up."

His arm tightened around her. "You are adorable."

Sublime memory caused a recurring flush of blood through his loins. "You are also... quite demanding."

"Me?" Her head twisted upward. Dark-fringed eyes revealed startled innocence.

"Yes, you," he teased. "We both slept for awhile, and when I tried to leave, you wouldn't let me go, so...."

"I know," she laughed. A smile wreathed her whole face. "We got all wrapped up in each other... again."

The overwhelming joy expressed in both her face and her words struck him dumb with pleasure. When he could speak, his voice filled with emotion.

"Rosina. How beautiful you are. How overflowing is your vitality; How deep the fire of life within you. I wish I could put into words what it means to love... and be loved, by you! "

"I feel the same... way. Together, we pleased each other. We... became one."

He pressed her head again beside his neck and looked out of the window at a passing village snuggled in the mountain valley. Abruptly, the train sped into a tunnel. A discomforting thought stabbed his subconscious. How could he have suffered this trip, if she were not here beside him?

All along the Blenio valley, searing hot sunlight beat down upon Italian-flavored villages and onto a train eating up miles of track on its way toward Saint Gotthard Tunnel.

Climbing ever upward through the Leventina gorge, Ward well understood why this country lived off electricity instead of oil.

Shortly before Airolo, Rosina pointed out the Riton Power Station which supplied power for this end of the line. "Because Siegwart furnishes most of the equipment that goes into these stations, I have learned where they are and what they do."

"Siegwart Company is the best thing that ever happened to me, " he said. His face was bright with enchantment.

She grinned. "Seriously, Ward. Do you feel that Colonial Power will award us the contract?"

"It is not up to me alone. I won't know until after the meeting in Washington on Monday. However, it seems likely. When you consider savings into millions of dollars, plus high quality, it becomes our responsibility, after studying all the estimates, to recommend the best possible arrangement.

Bells tinkled to announce dinner. Ward stood up, allowing Rosina to step in front. He turned to Stanley, "Come on."

"You two don't want me with you," came a glum reply. "I'll be along in a few minutes." He waved them off with the back of his hand, then turned to stare out the window.

Rosina reached over, touching his arm. "We do want you with us, Stanley. Please come."

They exchanged looks of deep understanding. Hers, of sympathy, his, of grateful pleasure. He could have fallen in love with this girl himself, had she given him one glance of encouragement.

Entering the diner, all three reacted to subdued light as the Gotthard Tunnel swallowed the train. There was only time enough to order, and have a bottle of wine placed on the table, before they burst out of its northern mouth.

After crossing a bridge high over the Gotthard-Reuss, the red demon slid to a stop at Goshenen, a gloomy grotto between two cold, gigantic hips. After a short wait while autos rolled off flat-bed cars, the train piped again and sped northward into the land of tunnel-loops, spectacular viaducts, and the roaring Reuss River,

To Ward it was even more enchanting than on the way south, for he now felt enriched purpose in his life. He turned his head to smile at the girl beside him. And she, full of her own illimitable joy smiled back.

Stanley—seated across the table—had become fascinated with the passing countryside. With the delight of a child, he kept up a running commentary. "How about that! First we saw that village on our right. Then it appeared on the left and we seem to be moving south. Come out of another tunnel and presto! the same village from a different angle. Whoever coined the phrase, 'Didn't know whether he was coming or going', must have been riding, through Wassen."

"These tunnels," Rosina explained, "were not built in modern times. They were completed in 1880. At that time, my great-grandfather Niclaus bought some shares in the Gotthard line at a time when—only partly finished—the commission ran out of money. He left them to my grandmother, Anna Niederer Wyler and her brother Karl Niederer."

"Does your family still hold an interest in all this?" Stanley asked.

"I don't think so. The railroad now belongs to the Swiss Confederation. My father would never talk about the monetary value of anything with me; a mere woman. He would speak only of the romantic part; the Niederers and their accomplishments. It is an obsession ‚with him."

At one point in this miracle of railroad engineering, brakes squealed as the train came to a shuddering halt. Diners continued to eat their dinners; talk; laugh; and admire a view of the picture-book village, dominated by a quaint church-tower—which was neither onion nor gambrel shaped, but a four-sided combination of both.

After a while, Ward looked at his watch. "We've been here, ... at least fifteen minutes."

"That is right," agreed a puzzled Rosina, as she glanced down the steep hillside flowing sharply to the valley floor. She looked across the aisle where nothing showed, but a solid wall of red-brown cliff. "This," she observed, "is not even the station."

The waiter came to take their plates. Rosina spoke to him.

"Ober, warum halt denn der Zug so lange hier?"

"Es gab ein Ungluck dort oben auf der Landstrasse. Ein Rad von einem Auto und andere Uberbleibsel sind aur das Geleise gerollt. Der Antliche Aufseher ist schon da, um zu shen, wie gross der Schaden ist. Es wird nicht zu lange dauern. Der Zug wird nicht spat ankommen."

"Well?" the two men asked simultaneously, as the waiter moved away.

"An accident on the road above, a wheel from an auto, or some rocks, rolled down onto the tracks. They inspect for damage to the rails. We shall go immediately." She then repeated the waiter's last words. "The train will not be late."

"You mean, they can make up the time?" Ward asked.

"Probably not," she shrugged. "Even so, the train will not be late." Casually, she picked up a wafer-thin cookie out of a vanilla mound.

The double talk so intrigued both men, they looked at each other. An amused, quizzical expression across each face did not escape Rosina's notice.

"Trains in Switzerland," she explained, splaying out both hands, palms upward, "are never late. Sometimes a little... delayed, but late? Never!" She nibbled on the wafer, and ate her ice cream.

* * *

On this same Friday evening, Otto Lander and Jeanette Bondt enjoyed dinner together at Hotel zum Storchen on the west bank of the Limmat. From the second floor dining room, seated by the window, Jeannette looked out across the river at Grossmunster, whose tall twin towers have dominated the city of Zürich for nine centuries.

"I have never been here before," she told Otto.

"You have lived in Zürich all your life and never been here?" he asked, thinking it incredible for such an attractive, single woman. "What <u>have</u> you been doing for the past thirty years?"

Her gaze centered on a group of black ducks. One picked fleas from the head of another. She wondered if, she should tell Otto about Willy. Since last Monday evening, when he had taken her to dinner at Baur au Lac, she had found immense comfort in looking forward to this evening's engagement.

On Tuesday, Otto had gone to Mannheim, Germany for labor discussions with directors of a subsidiary plant. He had arrived back in Zürich, only this afternoon.

Now he felt a compelling urge to know about her life outside of Siegwart Company. He followed her gaze, watched the ducks a few moments, then took a small package from his pocket. He handed it to her.

"Brought you something from Heidelberg."

"Thank you Otto," she said, with genuine surprise. Lines beside her mouth wrinkled into large crescents.

She opened the oblong package with nervous hands, and drew out a bottle of Madame Rochas perfume. She looked up into Otto's eyes, golden topaz into pale blue. He felt a moment of discomfort before he shifted his gaze to encompass her carefully coiffured hair, which glistened like bright sunshine, then down to a throat of pale ivory above the wine-red neckline of her dress. He watched the rise and fall of her breathing. With slight embarrassment, he glanced up from her full breasts, back to her eyes.

"It is a pleasure to buy things for a beautiful woman." Otto spoke with deep sincerity.

Tears stung her eyes. She could not remember Willy ever giving her perfume... or anything else, for that matter. She decided to tell Otto at the same moment he decided to ask.

He lifted his wine glass to drink the ruby liquid. His eyes above the rim watched her with profound intensity.

"Jeanette, the day I came into your office and found you alone, you had been crying. Would you tell me why?"

He set his glass down and... waited.

She drained her own and placed it on the table.

Otto picked up the bottle and refilled both glasses.

She told him only the facts; not a very pretty picture when looked at objectively. Only lovers see it as something remarkable, something theirs alone. Details were not difficult for Otto to imagine. He studied her face as she talked. Her grave eyes seldom left the Grossmunster, now brightly lit. It shone stark white, individual, in a unique position surrounded by fat, square buildings half its height.

"Are you still in love with him?"

The question surprised her. "I don't know... I... think so."

Otto could not imagine how this was possible. His voice expressed his irritation. "And what has he done for you, all these years? What has he given you... besides a broken heart?"

"Done for me? Given me?" She thought about it, "We were deeply in love, there was no... need." She went on in a quiet tone. "He never loved his wife. We were hurting no one."

"Hurting no one!" Otto blurted, raising his voice in anger. "Good God, woman! What about yourself?"

"Me?" she asked in a small voice, hardly more than a whisper.

"You must have known you were traveling down a one way street. Now that it is over, you realize that. Don't you?"

"Over?" she thought. How precise he was!

"Yes, over! If this Doctor does not care enough to give you some explanation, you should face the fact that it is over."

Jeanette had placed her left elbow on the table. Her thumb and forefinger cradled a trembling chin. Yes... it was over. She had known it for several months. Now for the first time she realized it with absolute finality. The trembling which had started with her chin now sent icy currents through her entire body.

Otto watched the transformation; from eyes of warm gold, to an absent vacant stare; from a pleasant, open face to a sober, hollow mask. He called the waiter, and asked for coffee and brandy.

Jeanette stared at the waiter's black bow tie, then turned her drained face southward, to look across the bridges toward open lake, stark and black against a glowing city. Uphill, off to the left was her apartment. She wished she were back there now... alone, where no one, much less, Otto, could see her.

"Drink this," she heard Otto saying. "You will feel better."

She blinked clouded eyes to focus on the cup of black liquid in front of her. Mechanically, she picked it up and sipped the hot, strong coffee.

Otto began to talk, pausing occasionally to taste his brandy. "Someday it will lose its importance in your thinking. You will shove it back in your mind and look ahead. It is no good to look back, Jeanette. Looking back makes the lines of age form too quickly. I faced up to that at Christmas, the first one without Helene. I realized then, that life goes on, and that I could no longer burden my children and grandchildren by being a morose, sad-eyed old man. So I began to interest myself in other things, and gradually realized how necessary that is to a person's sanity."

His words were good therapy. She had, in the last hour, been to hell and back. Otto went on talking; about his children, about learning to play golf, and reading books he had never had time for. She forgot about herself as they discussed new books, concerts, and the details of his recent trip to Germany.

"It is ten o'clock," Otto said, looking at his watch. He had become restless, and wanted to move.

In his car—outside her apartment—Jeanette asked him to come in. "I will be quite frank, Otto. Right now I would rather not… be alone."

"Never let it be said," he answered with pleasure, "that Otto Lander refused to oblige a lady, especially such a beautiful lady."

The compliment pleased her. She smiled—being acutely aware that a strange bliss had seeped into her through Otto's companionship. It made her feel good.

Those fiery eyes, thought Otto, as he followed her into the lift, are most appealing, and those inviting lips are damnably disconcerting!

She heard her phone ringing before she unlocked the door.

By the time she reached it, no answer came. "If it is important," she shrugged, "they will call again."

Otto noticed the avoidance of: "he."

She flicked on several lights then went over to Hi-Fi system in the corner where she sorted out records, choosing those which she thought Otto might enjoy.

He walked to the window—where a sweep of bright city lights spread out below in scintillating magic, except for a great dark spot to his left which was the Lake of Zürich. The strains of Strauss' "Artists Life" intoned quietly—at low volume.

"You have a better night view than I have," observed Otto.

"Perhaps so, at night. But you see more of the lake."

"This apartment," he said, looking around. "It is more sensible for a person living alone... to live like this, than in a big house like mine."

Before Jeannette could comment, the phone rang again. She went to answer it, and Otto stepped discreetly over to the pile of records. He read, or pretended to read, the small print on the back of one cover.

"Yes, of course," he heard her say, and then, "Auf Wiedereshen."

She offered no explanation of the phone call. Except for soft music, there was pregnant silence.

Otto had something on his mind—which had been interrupted by the phone.

"I was talking about my big house. It is too much for a man, alone."

"Then you should sell it; get something smaller."

"My children would not like that."

"Do you stay there just to please your children? You said it yourself, one must lead his own life."

"Precisely. Which is why I think it a good idea... for us to get married."

"To... fill up your house?" she chided.

His face reddened. "That is not fair. I want you... to marry me." He still shuffled records, looking at titles he did not read.

"Otto, look at me," she asked softly, as she walked closer to him. "Could I say, yes, to a man who does not take me in his arms, and at least... kiss me?"

"Ah, Jeanette," breathed Otto, as he quite willingly obliged. His lips found hers, while his arms enfolded her in a tight embrace.

She put her arms around him, fully aware of this unique experience which she had known before with only one man.

She moved her head back to look directly at him. His blue eyes twinkled with pleasure.

"You are delightful, Jeanette." His arms still held her in an arc against his chest. "I meant it when I said you are beautiful."

With studied intensity she searched his eager, glowing eyes.

"You want to marry me," she asked, "in spite of my long affair with Doctor Gottfried!"

"Rather, because of it." he responded.

"Oh?" she recoiled in surprise, and raised questioning eyebrows. Is that what he really meant to say?

"Jeanette, I don't want a dried-up old maid to share my bed. I want a live, warm, responsive woman. I believe you are just that."

She lowered her eyes as a hot flush of embarrassment flooded her cheeks. But Otto went on talking. "I won't rush you, even though, for my part, I would like nothing better…" He drew her head close beside his and whispered near her ear. "… but if you give me the chance, I know we could learn to love each other… completely."

Wouldn't rush me, indeed, she thought with sudden panic.

She stiffened a little and took in a deep breath. "When I am as certain of that as you are, Otto, then, I will marry you."

He kissed her again, and knew from her warm response that he would not have long to wait.

Chapter Twelve

At nine o'clock, a delayed train arrived at Zürich Bahnhof. Ward dispatched Stanley with their luggage across the street to the Schweitzerhof Hotel. He kept Rosina's while she went off to make two phone calls. Then, from a central kiosk, he purchased all the chocolate bars his coat pockets would hold. His father loved chocolate.

On the train, he and Rosina had made cursory plans. Because her parents did not expect her until Sunday, she planned to spend the night with Jeanette. She needed advice which—she felt—only Jeanette could give her.

The airport bus would be leaving Zürich Bahnhof before nine on Saturday morning. Ward's schedule was planned for arrival in Boston, where he would stop-over with his father in nearby Gloucester. Early on Monday morning, he would continue on to Washington. "I can change my flight to Sunday," he had suggested. "Then I could meet your parents."

"No, please... she insisted. "Believe me, it will be easier to manage the confrontation with my father... alone." She had looked away from him then, out of the window, and across the lake to the lights of Zürich in the approaching distance. "How I deal with Karl concerns me more. You cannot help with that either, but Jeanette can."

"Karl speaks English, doesn't he?"

"Of course. But this is _my_ problem, Ward. I have to do it the way I think best."

"And you will… do it." A shade of doubt crept into his voice.

Before she could retort, the words became stifled by an overwhelming fear; How? How could she possibly do It?

"It may," she answered, "take a little time, Ward."

Surely, he expected that, he could wait a few weeks. But, <u>weeks</u> was not exactly what Rosina had in mind.

* * *

He watched her now as she left the telephone enclosure and came toward him. "There is no answer," she said. "Neither Uncle Niclaus nor Jeanette is at home."

"Come over to the hotel. You can try again from there."

He picked up her suitcase and they walked out through the station and crossed the street.

She gave the phone numbers to the operator in the lobby. Then she and Ward went in to the bar to wait. Ward ordered scotch and water; Rosina, lemonade.

"The Champagne last night was too much for me."

"I thought It was just right for you, considering what happened afterward."

She swept him a look of secretive complicity. Her eyes sparkled. A row of white teeth pressed lightly on her lower lip. In that instant, he felt helplessly trapped by the pressure of leaving in the morning. He told her this, then added. "I could check with Swissair to see what they could do about a day's postponement?"

"That could leave you stranded. You might not make your meeting on Monday."

"So, I would get there on Tuesday." he shrugged with indifference. His eyes opened wide with humor.

"But you said, they <u>expect</u> you on Monday."

"Yes ma'am. Why I might even get… sacked."

His off-hand manner surprised her—even though she knew he teased her. He kept it up. "I have always wanted to go back to Gloucester, learn Portuguese, and join the fishing fleet. It is a thrilling sight watching those boats come in."

"If you do as well with Portuguese as you did with Italian.".," she mused, "we would starve."

He did like her use of, we. He could have burst with the pride it gave him. "Rosina, my darling, you certainly have changed."

"Yes." Her gaze was steady and confident. "Because… you fell in love with me."

A waiter beckoned her to the phone.

Not until she had left the table and disappeared did the realization of final good-byes drain the joy from his chest. Facing up to the reality of it, he drew a pen and notebook from his breast pocket, tore off a sheet and wrote out three addresses. He spent the rest of the time until she returned in profound thought. Avalanches, bombed airplanes, and other major tragedies; delayed trains and love, minor ones; were pesky annoyances to the orderly Swiss. Ward likened them to ants. When a crumb ten times larger is placed in their path, they hesitate but a second then merely climb over the obstacle.

A soft, quite familiar voice interrupted his absorption.

"Jeanette is home now," she said as she slipped into her seat, picked up the glass and finished the lemonade.

Ward handed over the page of addresses. "The first is my apartment in Knoxville. The second is my office. The last; my father's house in Gloucester."

She read them all, then looked up in surprise.

"Cape Ann? That is interesting. My first name is Anna."

"I like Rosina better," he said. "By odd coincidence, Anne is the name of my father's housekeeper. Also, there is a Mount Ann nearby, and a village called Annisquam."

"Hmn," she mused. "That last… sounds Indian."

"I'm sure it is. But they have long since disappeared. Though some of the teenagers there with their long hair and head-bands sure could pass for Indians."

"No real Indians" she said, with mock disappointment. "I do like the sound of Indian names."

"How about Keowee-Toxaway?"

"Oh, what is that?"

"A power station in South Carolina. No Indians there either, but it is a lovely spot. And by way of making you feel right at home, we have to drive through twisting mountain roads to get there."

She reached for her purse, opened It, and slipped the paper inside. Then with a deep sigh, she said. "Speaking of mountain roads, I had better go up one of my own… now. I did tell Jeanette I would come right along."

"We'll take a taxi. I am going with you."

After giving directions to the driver, Rosina settled back in the crook of Ward's arm. From that moment on, he had only a vague feeling of crossing a bridge and wending upward through lighted streets, for he held her locked in a tight embrace—alternately kissing her lips, her ear, her cheek. Between these desperate farewells, he managed to tell her of a two-week vacation—the first of August when he would be back. She had better have things arranged by that time, because he could not again repeat this senseless agony of separation.

The cab pulled up on Bergstrasse behind Otto's black Mercedes. Rosina told the driver to wait. Then Ward—with reluctant steps—walked beside her to the apartment house entrance. The door opened suddenly before them and Otto Lander stepped out.

"Herr Fairbanks" exclaimed a surprised Otto.

"Guten Abend, Herr Lander," said a ruffled Rosina.

"Ah, guten Abend, Fraulein…" Otto wished he could remember her name.

In the confusion, all that Ward could say to Rosina was a hurried,

"Bye-bye," then turn to accept Otto's out-stretched hand. When he looked back, both girl and suitcase had vanished.

"I will take care of that taxi," Otto said with decision, "then drive you back to your hotel."

Riding downhill and through the city, Ward was obliged to answer questions the eager Lander asked. "However," Ward continued, "There is one thing which disturbs me about leaving Switzerland in the morning...."

Otto had reached the Hotel entrance. He stopped the car and turned his attention to Ward. "And that is...."

"I would feel better if I could have met her parents."

"You... suggested that?"

"Yes, but she said, no." He recalled her words, "you will have to trust me."

"No problem," said Otto in a tone of mild rebuke. "If she promised to marry you, and said she would work it out, then... you should believe it."

Such complacency irritated Ward. He suppressed his chagrin by answering brightly, "Yes, of course."

He stepped out of the car and thanked Otto for the ride.

As he watched the black auto meld into the other traffic, he muttered to himself. "I've certainly got a lot to learn about the Swiss. The first lesson is: not to doubt their veracity!"

Like a mechanical robot, he moved inside, stopped to inquire at the desk, and filled out the necessary police form. Then he rode the lift, located his room and let himself inside. And all of the time, tremors of uncertainty nagged within his chest. Tremors which would not be completely at rest until the day she could write and tell him that everything was all right between herself... and her father. If, however... as he had told her on the train, worse came to worse, she need only telephone or send a cable to inform him of her expected arrival in New York. For certainly she could get herself a passport and be on her way to him. (If she had the guts to do it.) This last thought was what disturbed him now.

In many ways she was like a child. Although delighted, for a given moment by what she herself wanted—any reminiscence of her father, impinged unpleasant fear which haunted her eyes and tightened the nerves of her body. Even though she tried to hide it, Ward knew that facing up to him would be the hardest thing she would ever have to do.

He was relieved to find Stanley asleep. Though he suffered an inner turmoil, he did not care to discuss it with Stan Eaton. The intimacy with Rosina was much too personal to discuss with anyone. Stan could muse all he wished—as he had the previous night. "Three thirty in the a.m.! Well, lover-boy did you finally get to first base?" And Ward had answered, "Stan, let me give you a piece of advice which I have found to be quite worthwhile. That is… to mind your own business!"

Oh, he liked Stanley all right, but as far as women were concerned, they viewed them from opposite poles. Stan's liaisons were fun and games, with no more connotations than a casual dinner-date. Whereas Ward—whose affairs had been formed within the bounds of affection and could be counted on one hand—had expected his to culminate in marriage. Yet in each case, something had come about to prevent it; sometimes the girl's doing, and sometimes… his.

But now, to him, had come meaning so deep and vital, it was as though Rosina lived inside his own flesh. He cared not whether he ever went back to Knoxville, or Gloucester, or anywhere in the U.S.A. At the moment even his job did not interest him. Without Rosina there would be lack of purpose to his daily living. To be sure, he would love, eat, sleep, and participate in that expected of him. But the whole of it would serve only to assuage a void—for she was now part of the very fiber of his being.

He undressed in the dark, went into the bathroom, shut the door and flipped on the light. He reflected upon the last three evenings. Wednesday had left him miserable. Thursday had given him sublime happiness. And now Friday a mix-up of joy and elation, but also of... uncertainty and doubt!

"Damn it!" he spoke to himself in the mirror. "No more of this. She is mine. Hasn't she assured me of that? It is the 'good-bye' that has me up-tight. That's all."

Finally, as he lay in bed, he wondered if she had also given serious thought to the possibility—for when he was that certain of her, he had taken no pains to prevent it—that they could be bound even closer by the bond of new life within her loins. On that comforting note, he fell asleep.

Jeanette waited at her open door for Rosina, who hurrying on light footsteps—came down the hall toward her.

Inside, she dropped her suitcase and swung around to grab Jeannette's outstretched arms. "Oh Jeanette, I am in love!"

"Humn. I knew that the minute I saw you."

As the two women released their hold upon each other, Rosina bubbled on with excited eagerness. "I must tell you all about him."

"The American, Fairbanks, is it not?"

A look of incredulous wonder came over Rosina's face. She followed Jeanette to the sofa and sank down beside her.

"How did you know?"

With smug certainty, Jeanette answered, "A little bird told me." She added facetiously, "a love bird."

"Oh, really now!"

"To be honest, I admit to matchmaking. On Tuesday, I had met the American in Otto's office where we went over points of the proposal to Colonial. Fairbanks impressed me as someone I would like if I were twenty years younger. So... on Friday I arranged to get you onto the same train and into the same hotel. After that, fate took over. Sometimes fate needs just such a nudge." She changed her tone to one of command. "Now, suppose you tell me exactly how it came about. You shall also tell me…" She raised her eyebrows in mockery, "… what you intend to do about Karl Niederer."

"Karl, yes…" Rosina spoke abstractly. "For that I need your help."

Jeanette snorted. "Put me in the same room with him and I would slap his insolent face!"

"You would not. You are too much of a lady."

"Not always, I fear," she said with derision.

Rosina rose from the sofa and crossed the room to the phone. "I have to reach Karl tonight. He is driving to Lugano in the morning."

Dialing six numbers, she looked over at Jeanette—whose brow had wrinkled in odd disdainful questioning.

"Well… I have to… let him know. You see, I… well, he wanted to come… for the week end."

Beneath this silly explanation, Jeanette could hear unanswered ringing. "It is only eleven fifteen," she reasoned. Then added with dry scorn. "Those two renegades, Karl and the Uncle, are probably still out on the town!"

Rosina cradled the receiver and moved back to her position beside Jeanette. She pushed aside all thought of Karl and spent the next hour in effervescent outpouring of the week-long events.

When she paused, Jeanette laid her arm across the girl's shoulder. "You have learned a lot in a week." She picked up Rosina's left hand to admire the jade ring. "You have to live with yourself, therefore you have to make your own decisions. That is a very important thing to learn in this life."

"Yes, I know. Even though it is not… easy."

"That which is worthwhile is hardly ever… easy," reflected Jeanette. "I have a decision of my own to make and believe me, it is not an easy one."

"Oh?" Rosina asked with sudden curiosity.

"Otto Lander just asked me to marry him."

"How marvelous." she responded quickly. Too quickly, she realized, from the stern expression on Jeanette's face. Her tone changed. "You do... like him?"

"My dear child. I have liked him for more than twenty years."

"You just don't... love him?"

"When one gets to be fifty, it is time to think with your head, not your heart. I have to respond to this with reason, not emotion."

"Which means?"

"Oh, I don't know!" she answered with impatience. "What I am really trying to do is convince myself that Doctor Gottfried is a... selfish, thoughtless, contemptible scoundrel, who I am well rid of. Whereas Otto is kind, thoughtful, considerate and..." she sighed with resignation, "does offer me self-respect."

Before Rosina could speak, Jeanette went on. "Enough of that. Now we should be more concerned about that spoiled brat, Niederer. He could be nasty."

While Rosina twisted the ring upon her finger, Jeanette visioned various reactions Karl might employ—all more or less repulsive. "You, my dear, are the only thing he has ever been denied... in all his self-centered life!"

Rosina stood up and walked over to the window. Below her the lights of Zürich spread out like diamonds spilled onto black velvet. Far off to the left, streaked reflections cast yellow daggers into the lake. With her back to Jeanette, she spoke with sure conviction. "Karl is still my cousin. He would not hurt me... bodily."

"He won't need to hurt you bodily, you naive idiot. Surely you cannot ignore the fact that because of ridiculous, stupid machination, he has your father on his side!"

Rosina clenched her fists and spun around. "Then it is time to tell my father the truth ." Her eyes blazed with anger. "I am not a child. I am not going to be pushed around like one. Vati is not going to tell me what to do with my life."

"Bravo!" Jeanette clapped her hands in mock approval of a heartwarming performance. "This fellow Fairbanks must be quite a man to have turned you into such a lioness."

Rosina laughed aloud at Jeanette's intuitive appraisal. "He is… quite a man." she agreed. An expression of dreamlike absorption spread over her face. Tears of joy sprung in her eyes. "I love him so. I ache inside."

Jeanette rose from the sofa and went to stand beside the love-struck girl. Her left arm and Rosina's right arm crossed each other's back as both women turned and stared outward across the glowing lights. After a few minutes, Rosina spoke. "I also love Zürich. It will be difficult… to leave here."

"That is to be expected. One always fears the graduations in life. As infants we cry for the mother's breast when nursing is done, then long for the security of home when starting school, then the security of school when starting work. It is natural to miss each routine in life. But, intelligent people do not succumb to that crawling back into a shell. No womb in life is large enough to contain us once we move outside its sheltering wall. So, if you truly love him you will go with him anywhere he asks you to."

"Oh God Jeanette, of course. Anywhere in the world."

Dropping her arm from the girl's back, Jeanette went back to sit on the sofa. "I see," she responded. "And tomorrow you will go home and tell your father that, eh?"

"We-ll…."

"Well what? I'll tell you _what_! You won't do it!"

Rosina dropped her eyelids. Her lower lip trembled.

"And you know why you won't do it, don't you? Because you are afraid of him! You, a woman almost thirty." By showing disgust, she hoped to fire the girl into facing her basic problem. "You have a very convenient habit, Rosina, of not facing reality. You have lived so long in the fantasy that 'someday everything will work out'—you fail to realize that _someday_ never comes… unless _you_ make it happen."

At this Rosina stepped over to the sofa and sank down close beside

Jeanette. Instantly, she felt the older woman's hand run along her neckline, felt tender fingers through her hair. Jeanette spoke tenderly.

"Tell me, if I had not insisted that you go on holiday and you were still in the daily rut of never doing anything, how long, dear child, would you have gone on that way?"

When Rosina did not answer, but stared back—with eyes so like those of a hurt animal, Jeanette answered the difficult questioning for her. "Until the day your father died. That is how long."

Jeanette hoped the severe words would pierce Rosina's subconscious shell. If she was ever to make the break, it was now. Now that she had the best reason in the world for doing so.

Rosina—deeply puzzled by Jeanette's reasoning—answered stubbornly. "You just said that I was afraid of him. That is not entirely true. It is not him I fear. It is something deeper than that. I cannot explain it, but whenever I cross him my head begins to throb and I have a tremendous fear that something horrible will happen."

"Quatsch!" scoffed Jeanette. "Stuff and nonsense!"

Memory flushed an instant comparison. Translated, it was the same as Ward's; "Rubbish!" Her face fell into her hands. Tight fingers pressed her temple. Vibrations from within throbbed against them. Oh, what did either of them—or anyone else—know of the dormant apprehension that—like a jolt of lightning—struck both brain and body at thought of her father's words, "You do as I tell you… or…." What came after the <u>or</u>? Something awesome, frightening, threatening. Search as she would, it was too nebulous to come clear.

Jeanette eyed the girl compassionately. Then taking both wrists, she lowered Rosina's hands and pulled the brown haired head against her shoulder. "You darling girl, I love you as though you were my own daughter. And it would cause me great anguish if you did not take the happiness which is now within your grasp."

At the quiet reassuring words, Rosina relaxed. The ache inside her forehead eased its throbbing. She listened intently as Jeannette went on.

"I told you that I had a decision to make—which I will do in the next few days. Once I make it I shall stick with it. Now it seems to me that you made just such a commitment to Ward Fairbanks. Whether you made it under emotional stress or by actually thinking it out in a mature fashion, leaves some doubt in my mind. However, in all fairness to Ward and especially to yourself, you must take a firm stand and see it through. Beyond provoking your father—which he will get over—and suffering Rosa's tears—which are inevitable—what other dreadful circumstance could possibly happen?"

Even if Rosina could have made some response, an insistent "br—ing" from the telephone interrupted any attempt to do so. Jeanette stood up and hurried across the room.

Rosina closed her eyes and leaned back. Deep in thought, she heard only part of what was said.

"Yes...." A long silence... then a horrified, "Oh, no!"

Rosina's introspection stopped abruptly at the incredulous tone of agony in the older woman's voice. Alert, she strained to hear. At the next words—"Yes, she is here." Rosina jumped up. In utter disbelief, she heard, "Yes, dear. I will see that she gets home. Good night, Rosa."

Rosina held questioning eyes on a face turned the color of white clay.

"How did Mutti...?"

"They tried to reach you at Beau Rivage. The manager told them you had gone to Zürich. Who else would they call, but me?"

"Why, Jeanette, why?"

Because Karl was killed, in his car... on the way to Lugano."

"No!" she cried. "Oh, no, no, no...."

Jeanette was beside her in an instant. Strong arms supported the stricken girl, who was taller, though not heaver than herself.

"It is m—my fault," she sobbed. "He was on the way to see me!"

Lugano Holiday

"This is only Friday," Jeanette spoke to comfort her. "You told me he had promised to wait until Saturday."

"Y—yes," she admitted grudgingly. Her lips trembled against Jeanette's ear. Then with a sudden shock of remembrance, she drew back and turned widened eyes onto the amber ones, so near her own.

"Wassen?" she whispered, waiting with bated breath for the answer. "Was it near Wassen?"

"Yes."

Instant reflections pressed into her mind's eye. The black-roofed church tower, a green velvet valley, a sheer rock wall, and her own voice, asking "Ober, varum halt… den Zug…?" With a groan, she slipped from Jeanette's grasp and slid to the floor in a grotesque heap.

Feeling a wet towel across her face and her arms being briskly rubbed, Rosina also felt a hard floor beneath her back. Above her Jeanette's face came into focus. To herself she thought, "I could have phoned from Lugano." While Jeanette—rubbing the girl's arms with both her hands also harbored a guilty thought, "It was I who sent Rosina to Lugano".

In truth, neither was to blame. For the giant hand which stirs the cauldron of fate does not concern itself with minor directives from the millions of human manikins which move to and fro across the earth's surface. However, the power behind the hand must indeed weep, over the senseless suicide those very manikins invite!

That particular one—when drunk—had been a safer driver than when sober. An imbibing Karl Niederer studiously maintained complete control. But the sober one drove like a confident chariot racer; the wind in his face and his head in the clouds.

Even while talking with Rosina on Wednesday, he decided he would surprise her and arrive in Lugano on Friday night. Promises meant nothing to him. He had always done exactly as he pleased.

But the unforeseen had happened. His car flew too wide on a sharp curve; hit the guard rail; catapulted over it to strike the steep, rocky, mountain-side, causing a tremendous clang to echo across the valley.

Thickly spaced trees prevented it from careening further down the slope. One wheel—broken loose on impact—bounced toward the tracks below, loosening rocks and sand on its downward path.

Underneath his twenty-five thousand franc automobile, the last male heir to the Niederer empire—in the thirtieth year of life—lay dead from a broken neck: An ignominious end for such a descendent of the industrious 'Kaufman'; old Niclaus Karl Niederer.

Before Jeanette fell asleep, she lay in solemn darkness while her mind whirled with the intermittent recall of the evening's turn of events.

She had phoned Otto to take Rosina home, then made hot tea for the benumbed girl to drink. Allowing time for Otto's arrival, she picked up Rosina's suitcase and half-led the girl downstairs to the street foyer. After which—returning upstairs to her apartment—she telephoned Herr Fairbanks at the Schweitzerhof Hotel. "Although," she explained, "there is nothing you can do, I thought at least you should be informed."

The last conscious thought—which dwelled within her like precious warmth—was the secure feeling of having a man like Otto, of whom she could ask… such a favor.

Chapter Thirteen

At seven on Saturday morning, Rosina heard her mother stirring in the kitchen below. She got up, slipped into a dark blue robe, combed out her hair and went halfway down the stairway to the toilet room. A bitter taste filled her mouth—feeling on her tongue like the lining of an orange peel. Washing up and brushing her teeth did little to allay a feeling of utter helplessness. For now, it seemed to her more impossible than ever to leave Switzerland; to leave her father and especially her mother. In desperation she wondered what she would do and how she would cope with this new dilemma thrust so cruelly upon her.

Last night she had not had to face Johann, for he had gone with Niclaus in the police ambulance to Basel. Only Rosa was there to greet her when Herr Lander brought her home.

Rosa—seeing that her daughter was in a state of shock had done nothing more than help her into bed and urge some brandy on her.

Now, Rosina knew she had to face them both. She thought of Jeanette's words: "You must take a firm stand." and Ward's "You will do it?" Both gave her a surge of courage. If she could have a few moments alone with her mother? Perhaps….

Stealthily she went down the stairs and into the kitchen. Rosa stood before the stove. Rosina went to her and kissed her cheek. (A ritual she performed with both parents—morning and night—ever since she could remember.) Rosa turned, and in her saddened eyes Rosina read an expression of pitiable sympathy. But sympathy—regarding Karl—was not what she needed... or wanted now. And the sooner she explained this to her mother the better.

Methodically, she opened a cupboard door and reached for three plates, cups and saucers. "Mutti," she began timorously, "Naturally I am sorry about Karl's death, but I do not... mourn for him." She placed the dishes on the table while she continued talking. I never loved Karl. I tried to. But I could not feel for him what a woman should feel... toward a man."

Still avoiding her mother's direct gaze, she opened a drawer and counted out silverware. "Unless a woman feels...." At the sound of water running in another part of the house, Rosina paused. She knew that her father would soon join them for breakfast. She continued "... feels with every breath she breathes and every step she takes that she is alive and living only for and because of that man... she should not marry him." With nervous hands she placed the silverware on the table, drew in a deep breath and continued bravely. "I have met such a man, Mutti, and it is him... I wish to marry."

From behind she heard Rosa's indrawn breath. "Rosina!" It came out with a shocked, hissing sound.

Instantly, Rosina turned and threw her arms around her mother. Tears stung her eyes and welled out, dropping onto the thin white hair close below. "Oh Mutti, don't you know? Can't you understand... what I am saying? I am in love with a wonderful man, who also loves me. Of course I am distressed about Karl and sorry for the Niederers. I truly wish the accident had not happened. But in no way, could I ever have had Karl... for a husband."

Rosa heaved a great sigh. "Yes, my child, I knew you could not. But your father...."

Her sentence hung in air as she suddenly perceived; Johann himself—coming through the kitchen doorway.

Rosina wheeled around. Out of habit, she started toward him, intent on bestowing her 'duty' kiss. Within arms-length she stopped. For a chill went down her backbone at sight of his cold, blue eyes, set like tiny sapphires in a face so like a wrinkled chamois rag. No sympathy showed in those eyes; Only raw, biting, fury! A sneer formed around his lips, then—like a snapping whip—he flung at her crisp words of accusation,

"Now see what you have done! Gallivanting off by yourself... has caused Karl to die!"

She groaned inwardly. Then with undue patience, answered softly, "Please Vati, it was _not_ my fault.

His voice rose in anger. "No? Whose fault then? He was on the way to you. If you stayed where you belong it would not have happened!"

Rosina felt her fists double up and her toes tighten inside her slippers. All at once, came the realization that patient was not the way to handle him. In rising indignation she voiced the wrath within her. "If! If! My God! Why can't you be reasonable? You probably did not know it, but Karl always drove as though he was racing in the Grand Prix. _If_ I had been in the car... _with him_, what then? I will tell you what! I would also have been found lying beside him... dead!"

Her suggestion struck vulnerable nerves. His face paled and he could not hide his astonishment—due partly to her defiance and partly the awesome possibility that her body could be lying as still and lifeless as was Karl's.

Seeing him thus subdued, Rosina moved closer and finally planted her morning kiss.

Deeply moved, Johann sighed. "Ah Kindchen." Then in what he believed to be real understanding, he picked up one of her hands in both of his and spoke consolingly. Now you will have what you wanted all along... to be a single maid... for the rest of your life.

"Oh Vati, how you talk. You never gave any serious thought to what I wanted... ever!"

"But your mother said..." he dropped her hand and turned toward Rosa, who stood silently—conveying by a shrug of shoulders and splayed out hands that it would be better to leave her out of it. The action only confused Johann. He turned again to Rosina. One finger pointed accusingly toward his wife. "Your mother told me you did not want to get married."

"Now Johann," objected Rosa. "I meant she did not want to marry Karl." Thinking that she was helping Rosina, she went blithely on. "Rosina has a man... someone else... whom she wants to marry."

"So!" he burst out angrily, "you both keep secrets from me! My daughter sneaks off to Lugano with another man, and..." he sputtered in hate-filled disgust, "... my wife hides it from me!"

"No Vati! It is not like that at all. I met him for the first time... on the train to Lugano. It is true that I want to marry him because I do love him... very much."

Instantly, Johann grabbed the muscles of both her arms. His eyes bore into hers causing her to drop her gaze to the hard line of his sharply pointed chin. "At a time like this," he hissed, "you talk of... <u>love for another man</u>!"

Knowing of no other way to vent his anger, he shook her back and forth—violently—several times.

Rosina merely flexed her muscles taut. Inner strength surged through her body. Johann's words could not harm her. Neither could his grip on her arms. A tolerant smile formed around her mouth. "Yes Vati, I will talk of him." She drew herself up tall and went bravely on; "I still love both you and Mutti the same as ever. But now I have been given new direction. I glow inside with a wonderful feeling of vital energy. His name is Ward. And he has become the very core of my existence."

If Johann doubted it, he had only to feel the strength in her arms, read the determination on her face, and hear the resolution in her words. His hands fell away from her arms.

With slow, abject steps he moved to seat himself at the table.

Mutti poured hot coffee and hot milk into his cup, then into Rosina's and last of all, her own.

Johann stared across the table, watching it all until Rosa finally slipped into her chair. In tense silence—broken only by a ticking clock, Rosina eat down.

"Who is this man?" he asked, his voice a mixture of contempt and apprehension.

Rosina, who felt she had climbed the mountain, now settled down to describe the view. During the monologue, only twice did she falter; over loving... an American and living... in the United States.

When she stopped for breath, Johann spat out with curt bitterness. "You think only of yourself!"

"No Vati. I think first of Ward, who is to me, the most important. I also feel deep concern over any grief I cause you and Mutti." She glanced at her mother's downcast eyes; at tears welling out beneath the lids. She felt like being pulled into quicksand. Her parents, her culture, her ancestry, all sucking her into its depth. She thought of both Ward and Jeanette. Together, their encouragement was as a stout line pulling her to safe ground. She hung on tenaciously. "But, I am going to marry him and I hope to have children. The day may come when they will probably hurt me as I now hurt you. If that is my destiny, so be it. I have <u>made</u> the decision. It will not be changed!"

Johann and Rosa sipped their coffee and stared at each other over the cup rims as they listened to these strange mutterings from a once obedient daughter.

"My greatest sin," this strange girl was saying, "has been in not making my own decisions—myself—for too many years! And yours has been... in not allowing me to!"

She looked up at the clock, then pushed back her chair.

"I must telephone Ward. He will be leaving soon for the airport."

Even before she returned to the kitchen, she heard bitter recriminations bouncing like ping-pong balls back and forth between Rosa and Johann.

"No more of that!" she demanded in a strong, decisive tone. To which, both parents stopped in mid-word, as though lightning had struck the house.

Once Rosina had gained strength by such decisiveness, she went on boldly. "Ward is staying over until tomorrow. I invited him here this morning because he wants to meet you. And, because I want you to meet him."

Two pair of blue eyes stared at this strange daughter. Two mouths hung open in astonishment.

Ignoring their cowed manner, Rosina gave orders as she began clearing the table. "Mutti, would you make some of your cinnamon bread, please? And Vati, could you stay home from work this morning? Naturally, we must go to the Niederers. We will go there this afternoon."

Having cleared the table, she started to leave the room.

At the doorway she turned to address her mother.

"Where is Great-grandmother Rosina's cantonal dress?"

With dull, stacatto words, Rosa answered. "In the chest at the top of the stairs."

"Thank you. I intend to wear it… for Ward's visit."

She moved on through the doorway—to tread on light footsteps—and went up the stairs. She knew they would follow her directions. And they—too stunned to offer objections—knew it too. For after all—one is always polite to guests.

After receiving the phoned message from Jeanette Bondt, Ward determined to postpone his flight. A return call from Swissair informed him that they could get him onto flight 114 on Sunday afternoon. It meant arriving at Kennedy after 9:30 p.m. New York time. With luck, he could still get to Washington by Monday morning.

Stanley went along, with instructions to explain—if necessary—Ward's delay. He now moved down the aisle of flight 140, bound for: Geneva, Lisbon and New York. Finding his seat number, he edged in beside the window. He decided that any standby for Ward's seat could have the middle one.

His thoughts went back to the week's vacation. To himself he said. "What a ball. Wow! But," he sighed with resignation, "like all good things, it had to end... sometime."

Suddenly, a feminine arm thrust a boarding pass in front of his nose. A voice—dripping honeyed words—said, "Pahdon me, but Ah think you have my seat."

Stanley looked up at eyes like two dark chestnuts set in a peach complexion framed by shining black hair. Sorry 'bout that, he apologized—most agreeably—then swiftly moved out to let her in.

With unconcealed pleasure, he watched roundly curved hips inside a silver-blue mini-skirt slide over into the window seat. As he moved back to sit beside her, she thanked him. Twinges of delight sprang through him at the sparkling smile which accompanied the thanks.

In response to the seat-belt light, they fastened the belts. "You going all the way to New York," he asked as the jet abruptly started its taxi down the field, "or just to Geneva?"

"New York," she answered above the engine's roar. "Ah live near Washington, in Springfield Virginia. Ah'm going home from school."

Dark, oriental eyes blinked an invitation which had little to do with her spoken words. The girl—obviously, offspring of a World War II Pacific-based soldier—had lost none of her southern drawl during a school year in Switzerland.

Stan looked out at misty landscape as the jet picked up speed and roared valiantly upward high above the clouds.

He reflected on the remarkable forces of nature which inevitably produced attractive females in assorted colors, at appropriate moments. And, thanks to modern medicine, knew all about... pills. Ah yes, life was fascinating!

But, into his self-satisfied reverie came penetrating blue eyes and a soft voice which said, "We _do_ want you with us."

He looked out upon a world of glaring sunlight, over miles of cotton clouds to jagged stalagmitic peaks poking through. Yes, he sighed to himself. There would always be a blonde Bergit, a brunette American, or a black-haired mutant. But, a girl priceless jewel like Rosina came along only once in a lifetime!

A lifetime? A hundred years would have been a more apt deduction. For even while Stanley mused, far away over the Swiss Alps, the modern Rosina made her way down the stairs, holding up both sides of her Great-grandmother's hyndred-year old dress.

Earlier that morning she had pressed the heavy blue jumper, white blouse, and striped apron, and hung them at the open window to air. As she appraised the silver buttons on each side of the bodice, she realized it needed lacing. Rummaging once again through the wooden chest, she had yanked the lacing free, dislodging a yellowed envelope. Intending to toss it back in place, her eye fixed on a strange blue stamp; U. S. Postage. The postmark, partly smudged, conveyed clearly the year 1921. In old script, brown with age, the address read: Familie, Kaspar Wyler, Wallisellen, Switzerland. She wanted to read it but time was short before Herr Lander would soon arrive bringing Jeanette and Ward. So she had taken it back to her room and slipped it into a dresser drawer. Then donning the garments, she hastily wove the lacing around the silver buttons and tightened the bodice to a better fit.

Meanwhile, Ward waited at the entrance of the Schweitzerhof for Otto Lander. An early morning drizzle hung a misty veil over the plaza, turning the pavement black and the sidewalk murky gray. When the black Mercedes finally approached, he walked out to meet it.

Jeanette sat in the car at Otto's right. Ward climbed in back. "You remember Fraulein Bondt?" Otto asked as he steered away from the curb.

"Yes," Ward answered. "How are you?"

She turned—half around and reached over, offering him her hand. "That is a difficult question to answer this morning."

"Yes, of course,"

Heartened by her warm handclasp, he said. "I want you to know... how much I appreciate...."

"Jeanette is a relative of the Wylers," interrupted Otto. "She will... help you talk to the girl's parents."

"That's great. I need all the help I can get."

"They do not speak English," volunteered Jeanette.

"I know. Rosina told me that."

Ward leaned back to observe passing buildings five and six stories high which lined a main thoroughfare. He noted that blue and white tandem trolley-cars seemed to have the right-of-way. Gradually, they zigzagged ever upward nearly to the top of Zürichberg where houses became scattered between patches of dark green wood-lots. Far below, red-brown roofs of Zürich nestled in the bowl of a wide basin around a lake which stretched—like an enormous blue thumb—southward into the haze. This, he thought, is Rosina's homeland; this breathtakingly beautiful, amazingly clean country. An alien land, from which I have the audacity to pluck the girl I want and take her three thousand miles away. Away from her parents and... away from all of this.

Otto—following Jeanette's directions—stopped the car before a white stucco house with brown blinds and an orange roof. On either side of the path between street and house, a minute garden—blazing with red geraniums, pink, white, and purple petunias, cups of giant poppies, and yellow marigold tufts—filled every foot of ground.

"Courage," Ward told himself, as the three visitors approached the front door. Simultaneously, the myriad colors brightened as warm sunlight broke through the clouds above. He stared down at the dearth of flowers with mixed bewilderment. How should he act toward Rosina? What would she expect of him? How much had she already told them?

Now there was no time for questions. A door opened. Jeanette moved inside. Ward felt himself move along in the middle. Otto came in last, closing the door behind him.

A babble of strange language confronted him from all directions. He

---

Virginia C. Taylor 163

watched the two women envelope each other in an all encompassing embrace. Jeanette, a gorgeous blonde with a full, though youthful figure; the other; white-haired, slight of build, yet strikingly handsome. Then Rosina was introducing the Herr Director to her parents. Something in their manner reminded him of two Hummel figurines upon the mantel in his Gloucester home. And how different Rosina looked, wearing a long blue dress laced tightly across her breast. Huge white sleeves encased her upper arms and showed above the breast line up to her neck. Around the waist was an all-enveloping apron with red, gold, and blue stripes. Her lovely brown hair had been parted in the center and drawn straight beck, where a blue ribbon held a cascade of curls hanging loose on the back of her head.

The dreaded moment came. It was his turn to be introduced. His feet—seeming like two concrete blocks—somehow moved him forward. Rosina came directly to him and offered her hand.

"Good morning, Ward."

He had no time to read her face, for in an instant she swung around to his right and placed her left arm around his waist.

"My mother, Ward."

He accepted the small, cold hand which was offered. It felt like a piece of porcelain.

"And my father."

Another hand, wiry, hard, and... trembling. Without the reassurance of a firm arm across his back; the pressure of her fingers at his waist; he too would have trembled. Visions of what they all had been through crowded his imagination. It was—however—quite obvious that Rosina had already explained who he was and why he was here. He could not remain mute. He must communicate.

"Rosina, tell them that I am deeply grieved over the unfortunate accident last evening."

While she accomplished this, the old man's eyes—behind silver-rimmed glasses—never left Ward's. Gravely, he nodded, then motioned toward chairs and a sofa. "Bitte, nehmen Sie platz." They sat down.

The furniture—covered with dark tapestry and edged with carven wooden arms—consisted of two large chairs, two rockers, and a small sofa. Rosina led Ward to the sofa. Otto seated himself. Then Johann sat down. Rosa and Jeanette, chattering in their strange language—moved away into the kitchen. An odor of fresh brewed coffee mingled with that of pungent tobacco smoke—now streaming upward from a strange metal pipe on which Johann puffed. In fascination, Ward watched— half listening to the jumble of conversation between Otto and Johann.

"What are they talking about?" he asked Rosina.

"The weather. It has been unusually cold and rainy so far this year. Everyone complains."

I'll be damned, thought Ward. I'm uptight as hell and they are there calmly talking about... weather!

He wondered if Rosina would be as nervous meeting his family? Of course not! Why should she? They would be enchanted with her! He turned to study her face. Eyes—reddened by tears—stared back into his with solemn intensity. Despite a sweet perfume of lilac, the odor of camphor filled his nostrils. He looked down at hands which lay folded across the apron where, on one finger, the green ring shone defiantly for all to see.

He studied the silver buttons; the tight lacing—which did nothing to enhance her natural bust line. "That," he commented wryly, is an unusual outfit."

"This dress belonged to my Great-grandmother, Rosina Londi." As she talked, she turned to the table beside her and handed Ward a four by five inch picture. Except for a broader face and a sharp hooked nose, it looked much like this Rosina. "Over a hundred years ago," she began, "on every other day this grandmother walked from her village of Küsnacht to Zürich, bearing vegetables in a basket strapped on her back. Her brothers remained at home doing the heavy work and her sisters were too young for such a task. The Londi farm, seven kilometers south, lay on the eastern shore of the lake. At the foot of the Grossmunster she crossed a bridge over the Limmat River to sell the produce to Niclaus Karl Niederer, who kept a food store in the old Kaufhaus on the opposite bank.

In spring she carried asparagus and rhubarb. Later, when peas and beans were ripe, she brought those. Niclaus watched for her to come along the quay, then crossed the cobble stoned bridge to relieve her of her burden. By August, when tomatoes were ripe, Niclaus began to meet her somewhere along Seefeldstrasse. In the fall when grapes were ready for market, Niclaus with a horse and cart, went all the way to Küsnacht, arriving there at dawn."

Rosina paused, reached for the photo Ward held, and replaced it on the table. Then quietly, with strained effort, she continued. "Despite parental objection on both sides—for he was twenty-nine and she only sixteen—she knew what she would do. Before the snow fell… she was pregnant, so, they could no longer be denied the marriage which both desired."

Rosina glanced over at her father, then drew herself a little straighter as she turned her eyes back to Ward. "I am no less a woman, than was Rosina Londi."

Ward, entranced by the fire in her blue eyes, the determined set of her chin, could—by juxtaposition in time—visualize this Rosina, deep within body and soul of the one from long ago.

Otto—with the tips of his fingers pressed together—had listened in fascination to the simple story of the humble beginning of "Kolonialmarkt".

Johann had no need to understand the story told in English. The words: Londi, Kauphaus, and Küsnacht, were all part of the family story he himself had long ago told Rosina. "Tales which come back to haunt us," he thought with wan hopelessness. He should have known she was up to something when she chose to wear his grandmother's dress.

He did not like the expression on his daughter's face. He puffed upon his pipe and through the smoky haze saw a vision; a sudden remembrance of how Rosa had looked at him on the day they were married. He swallowed hard, nearly choking on a mouthful of smoke.

Jeanette had paused in the doorway until Rosina finished talking. She carried a tray laden with china, silverware and cinnamon bread. Directly behind her came Rosa, carrying a large coffee pot. For no more than a second, the two exchanged sly, enigmatic smiles.

Ward started to rise, but Rosina deterred him. "Please, sit still. You and Herr Lander are guests."

After half an hour, when all had been replaced upon the tray, Otto stood up and made an excuse to leave. Jeanette rose too. Both turned inquiring eyes on Ward.

In an instant he was on his feet. "Thank you, but I would like to stay." He turned to look down at Rosina. "That is… if it is all right with you?"

"Yes, of course…" Her face paled, "… for a while."

She then addressed Jeanette, speaking her native tongue. From the conversation, Ward knew he was the major topic.

Otto settled the awkward situation.

"At two o'clock I will come back for you. We can drive along the lake to Rapperswil, then later this evening, I invite you to have dinner…" he glanced at Jeanette for approval, "… with both of us. You see," he went on, "it is necessary for the Wylers to visit the Niederers in Basle. You understand… why it is impossible for you to accompany them?"

"Certainly. And I do thank you, very much."

"Until two then, Auf Wiedersehen."

"Auf-Wiedersehen," Ward repeated slowly, with careful accent.

Everyone smiled, even Johann. It was the first light moment since Ward had entered the Wyler home.

Late that evening, after returning Ward to his hotel, Otto drove

Virginia C. Taylor

Jeanette to her apartment. An invitation to come up for coffee and brandy had been eagerly accepted. In fact, he hoped to stay for more than coffee and brandy if she gave him the necessary encouragement.

"Take off your shoes and necktie," she suggested. "You may as well be comfortable."

"Thank you, I will," he replied, removing the suggested apparel and also his jacket.

She moved about the small kitchen, humming softly. Once she called out to him. "In the next few weeks, I may have to move someone into Rosina's job, for I am almost certain she will quit."

"You will miss her. She is… quite a girl! But," he added with a shake of the head. "I do not see the old walrus letting her marry our American friend."

Jeanette thought about it, then came to the doorway.

Otto liked the picture she made standing there, wearing a small white apron across the front of a dark green dress. In her hand she held a measuring spoon.

"That story about the old Grandmother," she said, "I have heard many times. Years ago when the Wylers had Saturday night 'Feste', and all were rather noisy and in high spirits, they would nudge each other and ask jokingly, 'When do you think the old couple first co'pt in the hay loft? With the ripening of the corn, or not until the grapes?' And one time, someone raised his voice above the din and asked the Grandmother Wyler, 'You are her daughter. What is your guess?' Then as loud and ribald as the rest of them, she answered, 'I do not guess, you dumb head, I know I am on June tenth born!'"

Otto, having experienced similar family feasts, laughed heartily.

"But," Jeanette sobered. "I never heard it told the way Rosina did this morning, from the heart, as it should be told."

Otto sprang to his feet, crossed the room and took her in his arms. "Are you also… a lusty Wyler?"

"No. My grandfather, Jacob Londi, was brother to Rosa's father Hans.

I guess," she laughed, reaching up with both hands to push him away. "… that makes me a lusty Londi"

She struggled to get free and the spoon clipped Otto's chin. But he held her fast and the effort of her hands became weak and futile.

"Besides being lusty, and… having the right amount of female acquiescence, I hope you are also a good cook."

She stopped smiling and searched his face. "Are you intimating that if I marry you, I must stay at home and cook?"

"Certainly not! " he answered quickly. "If you decide you want to resign, that decision would be entirely your own. Besides," he laughed, "The Siegwarts could replace me easier than they could you."

Her golden-brown eyes glowed in the dimly lit room. A musing smile played around her lips. "Thank you Otto. That is what I hoped you would say."

Self confidence surged through him and he bent to kiss her lips, at first lightly, then with increasing passion. As he felt her arms go around him, a spark of vitality coursed through his loins with fiery insistence. He pressed her closer with such force she gasped for breath.

The sound of a dropped spoon caused Otto to release her enough to gaze intently into her eyes.

"I love you, Jeanette, I… want you."

With unflinching awe, she stared back.

During this soul-revealing embrace, Doctor Wilhelm Gottfried telephoned.

Feeling hot blood flushing her face, Jeanette picked up the cold instrument with a trembling hand. The sound of her name from Willy's suave voice caused an already madly beating heart to thump against her ribs. Why now? she thought in desperation. Oh my God! Why this particular moment?

She listened to his rush of words. which echoed in her ears like resounding beats of a bass drum. Marlene! Married! Henrietta! Divorce!

Before she could assimilate the true sense of his words, he went on eagerly, "Soon, Jeanette, I will be free!"

"Willy!" she snapped, in a cold, harsh tone, "I have not heard from you... since January!"

"After what happened... in Arosa, I thought it best... not to call." He paused, as though phrasing words which now seemed completely irrelevant. "I thought it better for us... not to see each other again."

"You thought! All by yourself! You thought! What about me, Willy? Did you think about... me?" A compelling urge to hurt him fired her bitterness. "You put me through the tortures of the damned!"

Otto held his breath, overwhelmed by the fiery anger in her voice.

"Dear Jeanette," Willy spoke softly, "I am sorry... truly sorry."

His controlled tone calmed her. She began thinking more clearly. "I am sorry too, Willy, but..." She turned to glance at Otto, whose eyes had never stopped watching her. "I have decided, to marry... someone else."

At the sound of his indrawn breath, his painful, "Oh," she felt a stab of regret pierce her breast.

"Jeanette!" his voice rose loud and sharp. "You are not serious! You do not mean it!"

"I am serious, Willy... I mean exactly what I said."

"No! I will not accept this! Tomorrow, I will come to Zürich. I will... talk with you!"

"You will, you will, you will!" she shot back, with impatient repetition. "It is no longer what... you will! The past is done, Willy, over, finished! From now on I shall decide for myself, what I will do."

"Jeanette, Jeanette," he pleaded. "Are you forgetting all our wonderful years... together?"

"I forget... nothing! But the misery of my last five months, has been a remarkable antidote!"

After a four-second silence which seemed like four minutes, she heard his strained voice, in a tone of abject resignation.

Lugano Holiday

"Is there… nothing I can say to you?"

"Nothing!"

"Dann, Viels Gluck… Auf Wiedersehen."

She tried to repeat, Auf Wiedersehen, but the lump in her throat prevented it. She visualized him squaring his proud, German shoulders as he repeated the farewell. Only this time he said, "Adieu, my love."

The receiver clicked, emitting a dull hollow sound.

Otto came up behind—wrapping his arms around Jeanette's waist. Distraught sobs convulsed her body and she leaned back against his chest. Then she placed one trembling hand over his and moved the other up along his cheek.

The bitter pill of resolution became palatable only because of Otto's affection… and strength, which she felt coursing through her. He held her in warm protection until her shaking subsided and her tears were spent. Then he reached for a handkerchief and placed it in her hand.

"Otto?" she asked timorously, as her head pressed beside his chin.

"What, my darling?"

"Don't leave me… tonight."

"Believe me, beautiful lady, I had no intention of doing so." He kissed her forehead and pulled her body close.

"Will you help me forget him," she whispered breathlessly, "and make me… love you?"

With swift response, he spun her around in his arms,

He kissed a closed eyelid—salty from tears—then a hot cheek, and finally her ear. "With the greatest of pleasure," he promised, "will I make you love me." One strong hand positioned her head as his lips found hers, while his brain savored the precious thought. With the very greatest of pleasure….

Chapter Fourteen

About nine that night, the Wylers left Basel. Rosina drove because Johann felt unsure of himself in the speed and glare of night traffic. He sat beside his daughter. Rosa sat in back. A feeling of guilt which lay like a transient veil upon Rosina's conscience, suddenly took the form of a strangling cord, when after ten minutes, Johann broke the tense silence.

"If you had married him… he would not be dead!"

In no mood for intangible accusations, she snapped back.

"Perhaps not. But I might be!"

"What talk is this… riddles?"

"Karl was the type of man who could not be faithful to one woman. I could not have lived like that."

"Hah! You think your skinny American would be… different?"

She blinked the light switch low for a passing car.

"I do."

"When a man is unfaithful, it is a wife's fault."

"I will grant you that… for most men. Karl was different. He was… like Uncle Niclaus, whose affairs do not last very long. If Karl had had his way with me, he would have tired of the game in a few months and left me for someone new. I must admit I toyed with the idea as one way to be rid of him."

"You mean… you never… not once?"

"Never."

"Your mother told me this, but I could not believe it. Gott im Himmell! Twenty-nine! and still a virgin!"

Rosa broke her uncomfortable silence to reprimand her husband. "Johann, this is not the time!"

Rosina kept her own counsel. Johann muttered, "Humph." And all three fell silent for the remainder of the trip.

Inside the house in the dimly lighted living-room, Rosina handed the car keys to her father.

"Too bad about you," he said with derision, grating the keys between nervous fingers. "Swiss men are not good enough for you!"

"Vati, please. I have a headache."

Johann persisted, "I know not what you see in that homely American."

"Johann! Leave the girl alone!"

"Hah! Now my woman tells me what to do!"

"Only because you have not sense enough to realize that she is also a woman, _not_ a child!"

"I should get to the age of seventy-five," he bellowed, "to have women tell me what to think, and what to say!"

His eyes glinted like cold steel above the gregarious, aquiline nose. Folds of skin between crease lines of his face trembled with anger. Because of this rattled state of discomfiture, which so threatened his pragmatic convictions, he burst out in a fit of temper. "I forbid you to marry... that foreigner!"

Both women stood in mute, patient silence. Rosina stared at his pinched nostrils, Rosa at his tightened lips, his voice demanding, "Did you hear?"

"I heard," replied Rosina.

"Good. Now go to bed!"

He turned and stalked across the living-room, down the hall and into his bedroom. The sound of a slammed door echoed—like a voice of doom—throughout the house.

Rosa shrugged her shoulders, screwed up her lips in a mocking smile, then reached both arms around her daughter.

Rosina—relieved by the expressed compassion—pressed her mother's head against her neck. Her lips came at a level with Rosa's forehead. "He is very stubborn, " she whispered. "When he talks like that, it makes my head ache terribly."

"Worry not, my child. He makes a noise like the 'Windgelle' sweeping up the Zürich-see. In a little while he is—like the lake—again calm as a mirror. I shall warm him some milk."

Rosina followed her into the kitchen. In the brighter light, Rosa's black dress and single strand of pearls set off her tanned complexion—darkened by sun and wind. Her long white hair lay looped around a large gold pin at the nape of her neck. Looking at her, Rosina's heart swelled with affection. "Oh Mutti, how do you stand it?"

"Silly girl. I love him. "

Rosa poured milk from a pitcher into a saucepan.

"But Mutti. He is so stubborn! Everything has to be done… his way."

"Ja, ja, I know. It is best now that you go to bed."

"I will. But first I must phone Ward."

"He is a nice, considerate man, Rosina. But I do think you have not known him long enough to marry him. You should… wait a while."

"No. I have decided. I will wait… only until August."

"August!" Rosa's eyes widened.

"Ward is coming back then. And… well, it is like this. I might already… be pregnant."

Rosa clapped a hand over her mouth as she drew in her breath. "Y… you… and h… him?"

"Yes, Mutti."

"Mein Gott! My little baby girl!"

Milk bubbled up and Rosa snatched it from the burner. Turning around, she clasped her hands on each side of her daughter's waist. Each set of blue eyes stared deeply into the other's.

"It was good?... my daughter?"

In a rush of movement, Rosina pulled her mother close as tears of joy welled behind her eyelids. "Oh Mutti," she cried. "Yes. It was good. With every nerve in our bodies, we loved each other... for each other. Good, Mutti? It was perfect. I love him so much the very thought of him sends the blood coursing through my veins making my heart feel too big for my chest...."

Pulling away, Rosina put her mother at arm's length, clasping her hands on both shoulders.

"You are beautiful, Mutti."

"An old lady... like me?" She dropped her eyelids. "Go on with you."

Rosina lowered her hands. "You have never before... looked so young... or so pretty."

"Now your headache is making you talk nonsense. Go to bed!"

"Good night, Mutti."

"Schläfe du wohl, mein Kind."

Rosina walked back into the entrance foyer to use the phone.

"How'd it go Sweetheart?"

"Terrible, Ward. Absolutely awful. He was so young. You can imagine how desolate... the family is?"

"Sure can."

"Did you enjoy the afternoon... and dinner?" Rosina asked.

"Yes. great. We went along the river, past that bridge you mentioned, then south through Küsnacht to Rapperswil."

"It has changed some... during the past hundred years."

"That's what Jeanette said, that it was easier for me to imagine what it _was_ like, than for them. They are so used to the traffic. She pointed out the churches and other buildings, but said the old Kaufhaus has been gone for more than seventy years. Even I found it hard to visualize, seeing a uniformed girl directing traffic by pushing buttons inside a glass enclosed kiosk."

"Progress," laughed Rosina, watching her mother walk down the hallway.

"We came back to have dinner at the Dolder, not far from your house. Rosina, it was so beautiful there. Just as we arrived, church bells shook the city beneath us with incessant ringing, then later the setting sun covered the Alps with an orange glow."

"Yes, darling, I know." She heard the bedroom door open, then close.

"May I take you and your parents there for dinner tomorrow?"

"I will go. I am not so sure about my father."

"In other words, he disliked me."

"Only because you are American."

"And, because I come on the scene at the worst possible time?"

"Yes."

"What time shall I see you in the morning?"

"We should… go to church."

"May I come?"

"Yes, but you will not understand any of it."

"That doesn't matter."

"What time does your plane leave?"

"Four-twenty-five."

"We will come for you at nine-thirty. My father might not be too civil, but he will be polite. Later, I will take you to the airport."

"All right, darling."

"Schläfe du wohl."

"Whatever that means, I'll do it."

"Sleep well."

"I'd sleep better if…."

"Good night, Ward."

"Good night, Sweetheart."

Having talked with Ward, Rosina felt better, but her head still throbbed. She put out the lights and quietly climbed the stairs. In her own room—lit only by moonlight—she undressed and crawled into bed. Lying on her back, with her hands beneath her head, she reflected—in brief spurts—a variety of images thrust upon her over the past twenty-four hours. Knowing from past experience that if she could—by thought replacement—think of something else; something new and different, it would stem the violent pressure within her head. Thus she projected time ahead to the letters she and Ward would… LETTERS!

In one swift motion she darted from bed to open the bureau drawer.

By the light of a bed lamp, she lay on her stomach and tried to decipher the old-style German script. "My dear family. From the new country I tell of my life and happiness." The next few lines divulged such words as; "gardener, widow, house, and, beautiful Cape Anna." Further down, she figured out, "Landbesitz" and "Heimweh". One could mean estate; the other meant homesick. The names Caspar and Anna, her grandparents, seemed clear enough and the closing; "In Liebe, euer Sohn, Andres". Her head still pounded so she gave up the mental struggle and turned off the light.

In deep, exhausted sleep, she dreamed fitfully, not of the dreadful evening at the Niederers, nor of her father's crass remarks, nor even of Ward, but rather of… the unknown Andres, who had married a widow and lived in a house on… Cape Anna, Cape-Anna, Cape-Anna, Cape Ann. It ran around in her dream like a cat chasing its tail. She awoke suddenly. In a half-wakened state, she found her purse and rummaged through until she found the list of addresses. Beside the words; Gloucester, Mass. Ward had written in parentheses (On Cape Ann)

Fully awake now, she lay back on the pillow and prodded deep within her memory. Where had she heard the name Andres?

Through the open window came the sound of fighting cats, the perfume of Mutti's garden and the smell of new-cut grass. HAY! A Sunday in July when Rosina was eight years old.

They had all three gone to Walllisellen to help the Wyler uncles with the haying. After a noontime dinner, Grandmother Anna Niederer Wyler—carrying a long wooden rake across her shoulder—had started for the hay-field. Rosina ran to keep up with her. Long, brown braids bounced up and down upon her back. But when Johann saw his mother, he had taken away the rake, saying, "Eighty-year-old women are not to rake hay. Go sit in the shade." When he was out of sight over a distant mound, the still standing grandmother turned to Rosina.

"When you grow up, my grandchild, do not marry a Swiss. They are too bossy. "

"Vati says I am to marry cousin Karl."

"Stupid man! That is one bad thing in this country, everybody marries the relatives. Now my Andres, he is the one with sense. He went to America."

Andres, then was Vati's brother!

With insistent clarity like a half-forgotten rerun on television, Grandmother went on talking.

"Eighty, he calls me, humph. I am only turned seventy-nine. Run to the barn, child. Fetch me another rake."

After raking an hour in the hot sun, while Rosina carried piles beside the haypole, the old lady dropped her rake, straightened up, and with both palms rubbed the aching small of her back. She uttered a groaning cry, swayed, and fell across the rake onto the new-cut stubble. The child had run to her, stooped down, and pushed her head and shoulder over, seeing only opened eyes, staring upward. She waited a few seconds for eyes to blink against the sun, then held her hand upon the stilled heart. She tugged at her Grandmother's apron, and swung it over the lifeless head. When she reached her father, she had said simply, and without emotion, "Come, Grandmother is dead."

Later that long ago afternoon, riding homeward into the blinding rays of sun, Vati had said. "You see what happens when people do not do what they are told!"

In Zürich, they had not gone directly home, but driven instead to the old Grandmother Niederer's house where she lived with her daughter-in-law Albertina, and grandson, Niclaus.

With startling reality, Rosina now saw a long forgotten vision of the old-old Grandmother of ninety-six. Her mummy like face lay like a withered coconut beneath strands of grey white silk. Two sun-tanned arms lay out over a billow of white quilt. It was the first time she had ever seen her great-grandmother in bed. Vati was saying, "Your daughter is dead. She died of sun-stroke."

"And me," the old Roslna wailed, "lying here like a useless rag! I must get up."

"No! It is not necessary. She was my mother. I will take care of everything."

"I am not ill," she protested. "I just get a little dizzy… sometimes."

Turning to the child Rosina, Johann said, "Stay with her, while your mother fixes her tea. I must talk with Niclaus."

When he had gone down the stairs, Grandmother flung aside the quilt and said, "Come child, help me get up."

"But Grandmother, Vati told you not to!"

"I have to use the toilet, child. I am tired of that pan beneath my bottom."

Feeling the pressure of a thin arm on her small shoulders, Rosina supported the skeletal frame, and shuffled beside her toward the hall where the old woman leaned for a moment against the door casing. Slowly, they progressed into the toilet room until Rosina had her seated.

"Thank you child," she had said, between wheezing gasps. "You are a good girl. Now close the door."

Outside, she watched her father come up the last few steps, with Niclaus directly behind. "Rosina," he had said, "Do not close the door tight when you come from the toilet."

"But, old Grandmother is inside."

"She is – <u>what</u>!"

Instantly he pushed open the door to find her in a heap on the floor, her nightgown above her bony hips. Then, husky Uncle Niclaus carried the unconscious form back to her bed. Vati ran down the stairs shouting, "Rosa, phone the Doctor!"

By morning, she too had died. The Niederers were called from Basle. The big house became filled with 'Family'. At the appalling sight of each grandmother laid out, white and unmoving, Rosina had run out into the Niederer orchard where—lying face down in the rough, damp grass—she cried and cried.

After a while—realizing she was no longer alone—she looked up at the head of nine-year-old Karl; a dark form against clear blue sky. "Why are you crying?" he said with an unsympathetic sneer. "They were just two old women."

However, it was not Karl's words which she recalled in stricken horror. It was her father's. "If she had stayed in bed as I told her to…"—As I told her! "You see what happens, when people do not do as they are told!" Now, once again, through the death of Karl, came the guilt—like a wedge hammered further into her subconscious by her father!

"If you had married him… he would not be dead!" In that moment it became as clear to her as the blue of the lake when morning mists—like a thousand ghosts – disperse in brightening sunlight.

At the impact of revelation, Rosina uttered a startled cry. "My God! That is why I have been afraid to stand against him all these years!"

She arose from bed and went to the open window. Placing both hands upon the sill, she gazed down across the sleeping city; silent now and less brightly lit, for it was three hours past midnight. To a less familiar eye, separate forms could not be easily distinguished, but Rosina knew them well. Knew exactly where—among the clustered buildings—set the Schweizerhof, to the left of the Bahnhof Plaza. There, Ward slept. Less than a mile away. Tears of sheer ecstasy slid down her cheeks. Oh! if she could only fly! Slowly, her eyes raised up to view a star-lit sky. The awesome vastness of sparkling space heightened within her a deep soliloquy of new perception.

No longer did a constricting band of pain vibrate inside her head. A great pressure seemed to have been removed from that part of her brain. Was it credible, she wondered, that the headaches, which came after conflict with her father, were caused by a guilt complex brought about by the events surrounding her Grandmother's deaths?

At the tender age of eight, the intricacy of mind and death had merged lnto a narrow channel... to disobedience and blame! She herself, had been—in both cases—the hand-maiden of death! She remembered now how Mutti—aware of her morbidity—had served to blot it out by suggesting a carefree summer at Wallisellen, spent with the Wyler and Londi cousins. The irony that two strong-willed women had hastened their own deaths, had not come into proper perspective until this moment.

Rosina began to estimate the value of her own worth; part and parcel of the independent women before her—whose prime purpose in life had been to accomplish more work before each sunset than was humanly possible. Mutti suffered this same affliction to a lesser degree, but she also possessed the indefinable quality of little self-esteem along with a truly affectionate nature. Ward had made a similar observation while they waited for Otto Lander on Saturday afternoon.

"You get your good looks and compassion from your mother. Your practicality and... stubbornness comes from your father."

"Those are pertinent observations for such a brief time."

"Not difficult. Underlying all the politeness, each one of us was studying the other. And... you were a good translator."

"I did not tell you everything that was said."

"Not necessary. Cabbages and lettuce, guns and pipes, are the same in any language. It is how the vegetables are grown, <u>how</u> the guns are fashioned, and, <u>why</u> there are metal caps on pipes that make the only differences.

They had been standing on the front path between the flower gardens. With one hand, Ward held his jacket slung over his shoulder. The other hand held Rosina's.

Lugano Holiday

"I think I passed inspection with your mother…." He hesitated. "Your father made me feel that the sooner I climb into Swissair's silver chariot—and nevermore set foot on this hallowed ground—the better!"

Now in the dark morning hours, she thought aloud,

"I—like a stupid fool—let that silly remark worry me. But no more, my darling, never again! For I am now very much my own person!"

She climbed back into bed and hugged the pillow to her breast. "Oh Ward," she whispered. "You wonderful, precious man. Can I ever tell you what you have done for me? How I love you, love you, love you."

With her arms still around the pillow, she fell into deep, untroubled, absolutely delectable… sleep.

Chapter Fifteen

On Sunday morning, Rosina aired her bedding across the open windowsill while her voice rose in song, "The hills are alive—with the sound of music...."

She wore a bright-red suit and now smilingly appraised herself before the bedroom mirror. "Hi there, you beautiful creature." She nodded an adequate gesture. "I am pleased to meet you. Never before have I seen such a happy face!"

She hurried down the stairs singing all the way. Her mother and father were already seated—bent over the table eating—so Rosina kissed each in turn, then poured her coffee and sat down. Only then did she stop singing about thousand year old hills, birds, lakes, trees, and a heart... filled with music.

Without looking into their faces, she knew her father was irritated and her mother amused.

"Vati," she demanded brightly, "What happened to Andres?"

Rosa looked up in startled wonder.

Johann answered grudgingly, "Andres left home."

"Is he still living?"

"I know not. After the First World War he went to Holland. He got interested in bulbs; Tulips, hyacinths, lilies. He had a strong argument with our father about raising bulbs instead of all vegetables. We never saw him again. It broke our mother's heart."

"But he wrote," Rosina persisted. "He wrote letters. Did no one answer them?"

"Hah, he wrote letters," Johann answered with disgust. "He never sent any address. It was impossible to write back."

"He did not stay… in the Netherlands?"

"No! He did not. He…." Johann looked angrily at his daughter. Reproach glared from his eyes. "He went to America! The same as you… thinking only of yourself… not of us; your parents! Just like Andres, thoughtless, selfish…."

"Vati!" she said with patient dignity, "Each person must live his own life. If you chose to stay with your parents and Andres chose… to live elsewhere, is that reason to be bitter, as you were toward him then and as you are now, toward me?"

She watched his downcast eyes; his jaw chewing bread.

He had not noticed the letter beside her plate. She pushed it in front of him. "I found this in the storage chest. It is too difficult for me to read. I understood a little, and I think that Andres must have suffered too."

"This is from Andres?" he asked sharply.

She nodded. "Please read it to me."

His face became a mask of stony hardness. "Why?"

"Because," she fired back. "It states, Cape Anna! Ward's home is at Cape Ann. If there is some connection, if it is the same place, we might learn what happened to your brother, Andres."

Johann's embittered expression—because this insolent child had the cheek to not only unearth family skeletons, but rattle one before his very nose—now changed abruptly, to one of intrigued curiosity.

"The blurred postmarks," he said, studying the envelope, "has decipherable letters in the circle. See the S T E R ? It is possible that is Gloucester. The date is April 16, 1921."

Johann's eyes focused on the letter and he read it through.

Rosina finished her cinnamon bread and drank the last of her coffee. Then rising, she helped her mother clear the table.

After a while, Johann stood up and went to a shelf where pipes and tobacco lay. He filled a pipe-bowl, scratched a match, and lighted the dry pungent leaves. The metal cap shut with a snap and he strode back to his chair. Leaning his left forearm on the table, his other hand held onto the pipe.

"I remember Mama getting that letter in springtime. It came a few days after my father died of cancer. She let me read it, then she put it away. I remember her saying, 'Johann, as far as we are concerned, Andres is gone forever. Now, we must get on with the planting'."

He breathed a deep sigh for long ago regret and continued talking. "In this letter he tells of having left the Netherlands, employed by a Dutch couple, the Herseys, as their gardener. The first winter there, the man died. In June, Andres married the widow, a woman three years his senior. He states that she would soon bear his child, which he intended to call Caspar if a boy, or Anna, if a girl. "Humph," he added with snide disgust. "Small consolation indeed for our poor mother."

"As you can see, there is no address and no mention of a place other than Cape Anna." He pursed his lips, then added quietly, "We never heard from him again."

"I suppose," Rosina shrugged, "there is more than one Cape Anna, or Ann in the United States."

She had been drying dishes as her mother washed them, but now pulled open a drawer to locate a pencil. Then carefully drawing letters in the postmark, she made them come out even for Gloucester, Mass. She shoved the envelope back across the table.

"You know you could have printed any letters you wanted?" said her father.

"Yes, I know. However, I do intend to ask Ward."

While she finished up the dishes, she proceeded to outline the day's events until Ward's flight. Without changing her tone, she added, "We will be married… on August first… but that is a holiday," she continued with sullen ill-humor.

Then, as the impact of her words penetrated more deeply into his senses, his voice rose obstinately. "Last night I told you…."

Rosina had already moved to the wall calender and flipped up the pages. "July thirty-first, or even the twenty-eighth, would be better."

Rosa paused before emptying the dishwater, so as not to miss a word between these two strong-willed people.

"Verdamnt!" exploded Johann, slamming his fist on the table. "You women do not listen to me any more! The vote! That is what causes this! Now that you can vote, you women think you can boss men and… run the whole country! Next thing you know it will be the banks and then… the Parliament! Switzerland is on the road to ruin… letting women vote!"

Rosina, who had moved behind her father, leaned over, placed both arms across his chest and aligned her cheek beside his.

"I think you need not worry. This country has been doing all right for more than six-hundred and twenty years. And I think there are not many women who would have the patience to sit through a session of the Great Council or a Landsgemeinde."

"Women in a Landsgemeinde!" blurted Johann. "God forbid!"

"Exactly," said Rosina soothingly. "Men are so much wiser. It is far better that men should decide about the laws of the land." She kissed him on the side of his forehead. "… while we women make the decisions of the home… and the heart."

Releasing her hold, she moved away, out of the kitchen, and back upstairs to get ready for church.

Keeping her back to Johann, Rosa wiped out the sink, as she pointedly watched birds pecking in the garden.

"She is really a very smart girl, that daughter of ours," said Johann as he puffed on his pipe, and thought further about politics. "She knows that men are… smarter than women."

"Yes," agreed Rosa evenly, "she knows."

Seated in church, with her parents on her left and Ward on the right, Rosina watched him peruse the arched ceiling, the leaded figures in stained glass windows, the distant altar, and the pastor—on his raised pulpit—expounding German words, none of which Ward could understand.

She pulled a piece of paper and a pencil from her purse and wrote: Did you know an Andres Wyler, now about 73, or an Anna or Caspar Wyler, about 50?

He read the message, thought for a moment, then with knitted brow, turned to move his head in a barely perceptible, no.

She dismissed it from her mind and turned her full attention to the speaker's voice.

However, Ward's mind could not long remain inactive. Bits and pieces of thought began reviving in his vision as though looking into an old stereopticon. First—because it was so recent—he saw Johann proudly displaying his garden. Ward pictured how crowded the cabbage and lettuce rows would be when fully grown. In bi-location he saw himself—a little boy standing beside his father appraising their "Victory Garden" during World War II. Dad, who had never raised a vegetable garden, got help from the man next door.

"That Andy," his father said, "knows all about flowers, but look at the way he crowds the vegetables."

"But Dad, that's the way he always raises them in the garden behind his house."

Andy—though taller and huskier—did remind him of Rosina's father and the gardens were so... similar. But Andy's last name was Vialor, and he was Dutch. He looked again at the names she had written. Anna or Caspar. He closed his eyes. Queer, how she had written or. Andy had twin children; Annie Carter, who had been widowed during the war and since Mother's death, cook and housekeeper for Dad—and Cass, who was married to Ward's sister Jean. Cass was not a proper name. What in hell was it, really?

He pondered. Then remembered her wedding invitations. He was sixteen. How he had laughed, ridiculing the name Caspar. At the time he teased his sister mercilessly.

Now, how did Rosina come up with such names? So co-incidental with those people; next-door neighbors and close family friends for as long as he could remember? In perplexed wonder, he glanced sideways at three roman noses; Johann's being the most pronounced. All pointed straight ahead toward the distant pulpit.

Another picture, much more recent, dropped into Ward's steriopticon vision. He saw and heard, Rosina introduce the Wylers to Otto Lander. She pronounced the name with a V, instead of the W sound she used when speaking in English.

The speaker's voice finished and the shuffling congregation stood to sing; "A Mighty Fortress Is Our God." Ward sang what he could remember of its words in English.

Outside the church, he turned to Rosina and asked eagerly, "In German, pronounce your last name."

"Vi e ler."

Her parents had preceded them down the stone steps and now moved toward their car. Ward and Rosina—with mounting excitement—began exchanging their vital information.

In the back seat of the Wyler car—curving up the mountain to the Dolder Grand Hotel—they continued asking each other questions until they knew with absolute certainty that Andy was indeed Johann's brother <u>and</u> Cass and Annie were first cousins to Rosina.

As soon as they were seated before one of the restaurant's wide circular windows, Rosina began translating. Ward's attention alternated between the Wyler's expression of suffused wonder and the sweeping panorama of scintillating perfection.

Below, tiny white buildings sparkled on a dark green velvet-like carpet, giving way to the lake and sky of azure blue, separated by jagged peaks looking like white caps on a giant ocean.

A white-jacketed waiter took their order. All agreed on curried chicken. Ward ordered a bottle of Dézelez.

"How many grandchildren?" was the first question Rosina translated for her mother.

Ward held up four fingers. He told Rosina, "Two boys in high school and two girls, eight and ten."

"For whom you bought the blouses!" she exclaimed.

"That's right. Here in Zürich I bought watches for the boys. The toy autos are for my sister Shirley's small boys. They live in nearby Annisquam. Cass and Jean own a motel they built on some of Andy's property. Originally he had more than fifteen acres. His house—a large, gray-shingled one—stands between the motel and Dad's property. Only a highway comes between the houses and the rocky Atlantic shore."

"Did he never talk of Switzerland or his home, or of his family?" Rosina translated for her father.

"Not to me. I never heard him speak German. When his wife was alive, they sometimes spoke Dutch. We assumed they were."

"Do Annie and Cass look at all like me?" This was Rosina's own question.

"No. They have light blue eyes and smooth flaxen hair. Cass is tall and muscular. Annie is buxom and quite jolly. As soon as I get to New York tonight, I will call Dad. I'm sure one of them will write to you immediately."

Dinner was served. The waiter offered the wine to Ward for tasting, then poured it all around.

Picking up his glass and looking directly at Johann, Ward said, "If he will come, I will bring Andy when I come back."

Rosina, overcome with emotion, took a sip as tears flooded her eyes. She translated for her father.

Johann's eyes also clouded with tears. Half rising, he reached out to shake Ward's hand in both of his own. The warmth of feeling which spread from one man to the other—along with the understanding which flowed from each other's eyes—needed no verbal translation.

At sight of Johann's rapt face, the two women exchanged smiles charged with the loving air of female conspiracy.

At three o'clock, Rosina and Ward left the Wyler home for the drive to Kloten Airport. She headed north along Frohburgstrasse and onto route one. She wanted to show him what was left of the Wallisellen farm where Andy had lived. Without descending to the valley floor, she stopped the car on a rise where they could look easterly toward distant farms.

As Ward took pictures, he commented. "This country looks like its inhabitants sweep every inch of it… daily!"

Spread out below lay rich, green farm-land through which the Glatt river wiggled like a writhing snake. "We have no time to go closer," she said. "It would mean introduction to distant relatives, and believe me, in Switzerland, the welcome could go on for hours!"

Ward laughed and they climbed back into the car. He drew her into his arms. "I may not be able to kiss you at the Airport the way I want to…."

Their lips joined and held for a long kiss, from which neither wished to withdraw. Finally Ward pulled away to hold her head close and whisper in her ear. "Shakespeare was wrong. Parting is not sweet sorrow. In truth it is a tormenting agony." He released her then, enough to look into her eyes. They exchanged a consuming gaze of mutual commiseration.

"Rosina, I've been in love with you for exactly eight days and now I don't know how I will ever get through the next forty-eight without you."

"Forty-eight?"

"Yes darling, I've counted them."

She pulled away from him and placed a thumb and finger on the ignition key. She spoke matter-of-factly.

"We had better go to the Airport."

While she drove, Rosina told him of the night's revelations which had given her a new sense of independence. "Now I no longer see my father as a tyrant. I see the man he is, saddened by each tragedy or disappointment in life, and not ever knowing how—except by domination—to make things come right for him."

"Makes me feel like a kidnapper, taking you so far away."

She turned into the Airport parking lot, pulled into a free place, then turned off the key and looked into his eyes.

"The Bible says, 'For this cause, thou shalt leave father and mother. Man and wife shall be one flesh'."

"Your father and mother would be happier if this particular flesh were Swiss."

"Well," she said, reaching over to kiss one cheek, as she stroked her fingers upon the other. "… even so, it is… awfully nice flesh."

"Oh God!" he said, grabbing the hand and kissing her palm.

Instantly they were holding each other close as tears threatened stinging eyelids.

"Oh Ward, I am so glad you stayed over."

"Me too."

He looked at his watch. "I had better check in. We can talk more in the passengers' lounge."

In a short while, they stood before huge glass windows—tightly gripping each other's hand. Ward looked down on Rosina who seemed mesmerized by long, silvery-white planes lined up outside.

She spoke like an automaton. "I forgot to tell you, August first is a holiday. Barring legal difficulties, we could be married a day or two before."

"I'll get back as soon as possible, for what ever has to be done. By the way, what's the holiday?"

She turned to look up at him. Her eyes glistened with tears. "It is our day of... Independence."

"You, my precious girl, have just had your day of independence. I sensed it in you even before we went in to church this morning."

Overcome with pride and elation, she nodded her head. By compressing her lips tight, she restrained a burst of tears.

Ward sensed that he had better change the subject. He spoke of how—at dinner—her father's attitude had changed.

"Yes, it has. He was so intrigued by your offer to bring his brother here, he was truly... overwhelmed. Which, I assure you, is quite unusual for my father."

"Which means," he chided her, " that when an outsider does something for a Swiss, he suddenly becomes... a friend?"

"Of course," she laughed, "like taking them to dinner, and sending roses, and..." she looked down at the ring on her finger, "... giving them presents."

"If that is the case, I had better do something for Mr. Lander. He gave me a rather condescending feeling. He was certainly gracious about everything, yet I sensed it was either because of you and Jeanette, or probably because of the Colonial project. And not... for myself."

"The Swiss," she explained with a smug all-knowing expression, "are not very demonstrative. It takes time for you to realize whether or not they do like you. The situation you will have no doubt about is... when they do not!"

Ward's flight was called. Passengers migrated toward the roped-off entrance line. Ward and Rosina—holding both hands—faced each other in a state of shock. Silently, each conveyed to the other a feeling of necessary courage, yet fully aware that clocks do not stop and planes do not wait.

The loud-speaker blared its final call—first in German, which made Rosina aware before Ward.

"Darling, you must go!"

"I know, my love, I know," came his agonized response. He hugged her quickly, then hurried off through the doorway.

As he went out toward the plane—wind flapping his jacket and pants—she recalled their last night in Lugano. Then too, he had whispered, "I know, my love, I know."

At the stair-way ramp he turned to wave, then disappeared up the tunnel of steps. Rosina stared for interminable minutes as the ramps were rolled away and all entrances of the giant plane were closed.

In vain she searched the window spaces set into a long red strip. Tears washed down her face. The red strip became a blur merging into the small blank squares. Above it, black words "Swissair" danced in glaring sunlight. She stood transfixed—waving a white handkerchief—until the plane taxied and turned its monstrous red tail defiantly in her face.

Slowly at first the jet moved away, then—like a guided missile—it raced downfield and finally zoomed, with a frightening roar to lift gracefully above the ground. For a moment, yellow sunshine glistened—like a reflecting mirror—upon its shiny surface. When it became a tiny thing, no larger than a silver bullet, she turned away.

With as much volition as a sleep-walker, she left the terminal and returned to her father's car.

Before turning on the ignition, she dried her eyes and blew her nose. Mentally, she thought of the days ahead. Tomorrow she must attend Karl's funeral. This coming week she would have to apply for a passport and give Jeanette a letter of resignation. The biggest obligation—which until this moment she had given no thought at all—was the necessary preparation for a wedding!

"Liebe Gott!" she exclaimed aloud. "A wedding! Then to America!... with... the man I love."

POSTSCRIPT

In the summer of 2001, four persons arrived at Kloten airport. They were Ward and Rosina Fairbanks with their 29 year old twins, Robert and Helene. Robert had graduated from Georgia Tech in Atlanta, and was employed at the Oak Ridge National Laboratories in Tennessee. Helene, a registered nurse, was to be married to a physician in the fall.

Rosina's last trip to her homeland had been to attend her mother's funeral in 1980. Her father had passed away a year earlier. She had faithfully fulfilled her promise of annual visits, except the year the twins were born.

At their arrival, Rosina explained that now an underground train transported the passengers directly into Zürich's station, the Bahnhof.

They stayed for one night at the Schweitzerhof. Dinner that evening had been at the invitation of Jeanette and Otto. The following morning they took the train to Lugano.

Jeanette had informed Rosina that the Beau Rivage was no longer a hotel, because it had become an apartment house. So she had suggested making reservations at the nearby Eden Hotel. Also, that pollution had so overtaken the lake, swimming was restricted to pools. There were other changes which surprised the returning couple. The traffic was so intense that pedestrian tunnels had become necessary beneath the main boulevard beside the lake. Also that concerts were now held on Sunday mornings, usually in the Municipal courtyard.

However, the views of lake and mountain had been unaltered by time, and the funiculars to Monte Brè and San Salvatore unchanged. Swimming in the Eden's pool was hardly different than the pool in their back yard in Knoxville, Tennessee, except for the backdrop of lake and mountain.

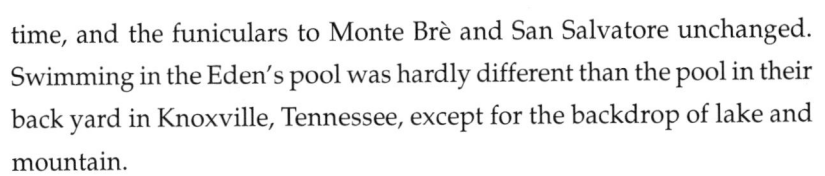

On the last night of their week in Lugano, as Ward and Rosina stood on the terrace east of the Hotel, Rosina smiled her enigmatic smile and said, "Our children have enjoyed it, especially the rides on the lake steamers and the visit to Miniatur, that Swiss village in Melide, and of course the evening discos." She then looked up directly at Ward and continued, "It doesn't matter really, because we will always treasure our memory of how it was."

Ward hugged her to him, and kissed her passionately, for nothing had changed their love and desire for each other in all of the thirty years of their marriage.

ISBN 155395825-X